Sew
SCANDINAVIAN

35 stylish projects to stitch

Kajsa Kinsella

CICO BOOKS
LONDON NEW YORK

For my husband and children, with all my love and admiration.

Published in 2015 by CICO Books
an imprint of Ryland Peters & Small Ltd
20–21 Jockey's Fields, London WC1R 4BW
341 E 116th St, New York NY 10029

www.rylandpeters.com

10 9 8 7 6 5 4 3 2 1

A CIP catalogue record for this book is available from the Library of Congress and the British Library.

ISBN: 981 1 78249 241 2

Printed in China

Editor: Sarah Hoggett
Designer: Geoff Borin
Photographer: Penny Wincer
Step by step photography: Kajsa Kinsella
Stylist: Nel Haynes
Illustrator: Stephen Dew

In-house editor: Miriam Catley
Art director: Sally Powell
Production controller: Mai-Ling Collyer
Publishing manager: Penny Craig
Publisher: Cindy Richards

CONTENTS

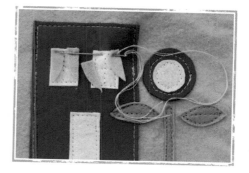

INTRODUCTION

Growing up in southern Sweden in a very creative family of six, I was constantly fed with visual ideas, techniques, materials, and design challenges. My sisters and I were never ever bored; with the fantastic Scandinavian natural world literally on our doorstep, there was always something to make or do and we used what we could find outside to build tree houses, go on excursions, and play games. The winters were as ice cold as the summers were hot—and even though my fingers still suffer from frostbite every now and then, my fascination for snow will remain for life. All the seasons of Scandinavia are vividly individual and so beautiful that it is not hard to see where the inspiration for all our beautiful patterns, color combinations, and designs comes from. Just fight the mosquitoes long enough to watch the sun go down over those rolling northern hills and you'll know instantly what I mean.

One of my absolute favorite pastimes when I visit Sweden now is to root through every flea market going for those distinctly Nordic fabrics and notions. We sure do love our pale stripes, Dala horses, braided hearts, and retro patterns! Over centuries Scandinavia has developed a distinct and unique style, which anyone can spot as being Nordic in an instant.

To celebrate the launch of this book, I have brought to life an old dream of mine— to create my own range of Scandinavian handmade interior decorations and useful items for around the home. My hope with this book is that you, too, will discover or re-discover a passion for all things Nordic. My projects are made to be easy to follow, and with only a little bit of practice you should be well able to create your very own Scandi-style home.

Enjoy and welcome to my Northern world!

Chapter 1 THE HOME

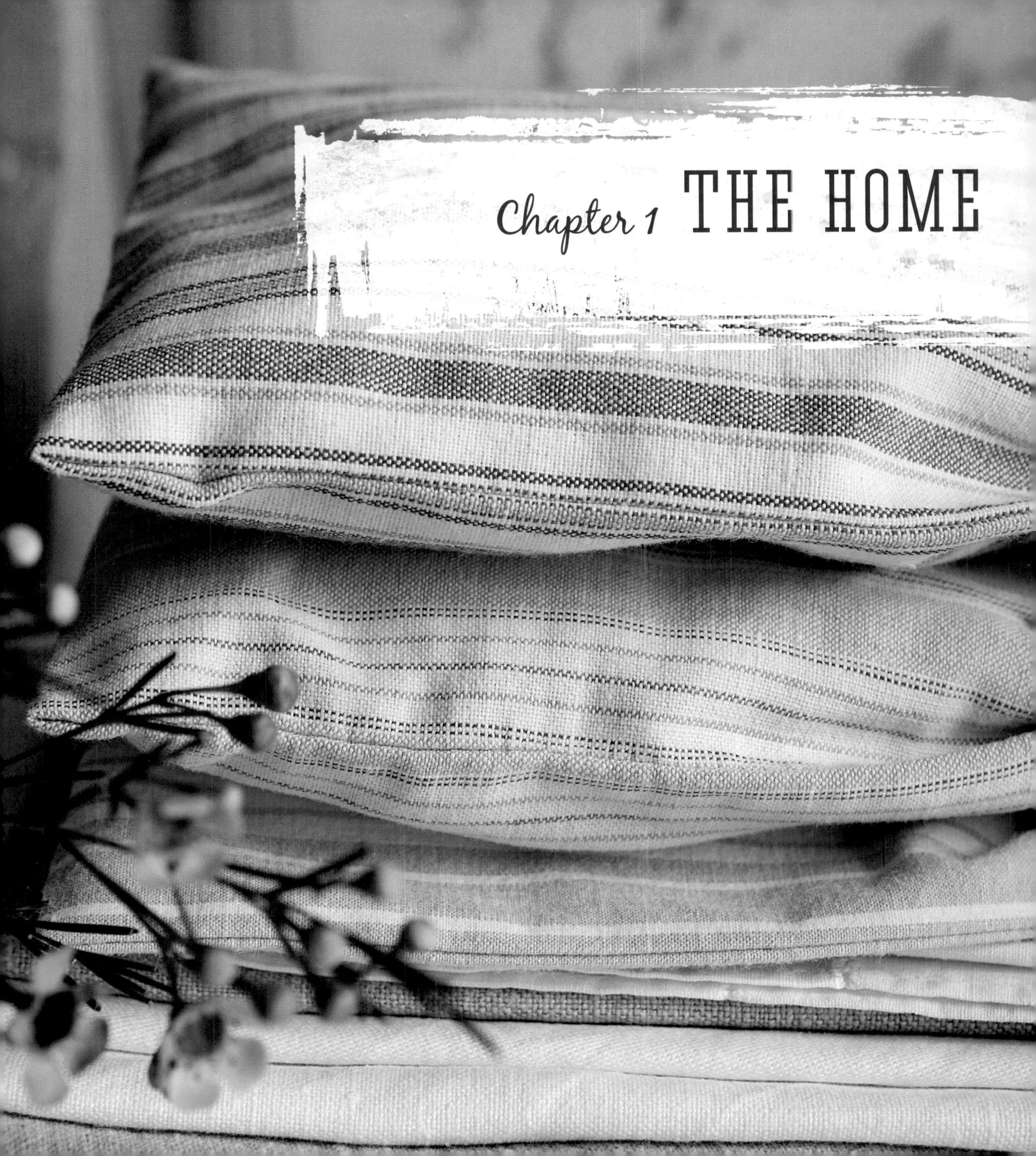

Arabia-inspired TABLE RUNNER

As the oldest manufacturer of pottery, earthenware, and porcelain in Finland, Arabia is deservedly famous throughout Scandinavia and the world. Founded in 1873, it has given us heaps of gorgeously designed crockery. The ones I love the most are the white and blue types, and here I have made an attempt to create a mid-century design of my own in Arabia style.

1 On all four sides of the linen fabric, fold over a double ⅜-in. (1-cm) hem and press well. Machine stitch around all four sides.

YOU WILL NEED

- 15 x 43 in. (38 x 109 cm) natural linen fabric
- 13¾ x 13¾ in. (35 x 35 cm) dark blue-and-white polka-dot fabric
- Dark blue embroidery floss (thread)
- White sewing thread
- Basic kit (see page 120)

2 Along each of the two short edges, embroider three dark-blue "crosses." Start with the middle cross: the center circle should sit 6¾ in. (17 cm) in from the side edges and 2 in. (5 cm) from up the bottom edge and should be ⅜ in. (1 cm) in diameter. Sew the circles in satin stitch (see page 121) and the lines connecting them in straight stitch, leaving 1 in. (2.5 cm) between the bottom circle and the bottom edge of the linen. Position the remaining two crosses centrally between the side edge and the center cross.

3 Cut out four circles of dark blue-and-white polka-dot fabric about 3 in. (8 cm) in diameter, trying to position the dots in the same place on each circle.

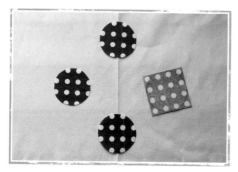

4 Fold the linen in half widthwise and press with a hot iron to mark the center. Place two circles on the center crease, 1¼ in. (3 cm) from the long edges, and the remaining two circles in between them, 1½ in. (4 cm) from the center crease.

5 Thread your machine with white sewing thread and carefully stitch around the edge of each circle.

TOP TIP

Stitch slowly, as close to the circle edge as possible, taking care to keep your stitching in a neat circle.

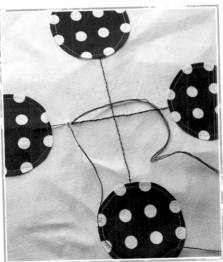

6 Using the same shade of dark blue embroidery floss that you used earlier and following the ironed crease line, sew a line of straight stitches between the two circles nearest the long edges of the runner. Repeat between the two remaining circles. Press the linen carefully—it's a gorgeous fabric, but it creases really easily!

NORDIC *mugwarmers and coasters*

Imagine coming back from a brisk morning walk in either the deep and majestic forests or by the ancient and rugged Scandinavian seaside, and being offered a warming cup of something steaming hot in a large mug! Mmmm—there's nothing better! Here I have created the perfect accompaniment to that experience—a set of very Nordic-looking mugwarmers with matching coasters.

1 There are some lovely gingham colors out there and I found four cheery shades for this fresh and summery project. Following the manufacturer's instructions, back each gingham with iron-on interfacing to make it a bit more sturdy and easier to work with.

YOU WILL NEED

- Templates on page 122
- 10–12-in. (25–30-cm) square each of green, pink, blue, and yellow gingham fabric
- 10 in. (25 cm) pale natural cotton calico, 36 in. (90 cm) wide
- 20–25-in. (50–60-cm) square of iron-on interfacing
- 20-in. (50-cm) length each of green, pink, blue, and yellow gingham ribbon, ⅜ in. (1 cm) wide
- White sewing thread
- Tweezers (optional)
- Glue stick
- Basic kit (see page 120)

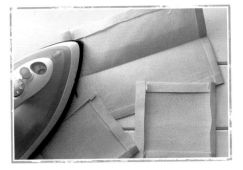

3 Trace the templates on page 122 onto white copy or parchment paper and cut out. Using the photo as a guide, cut out all the gingham pieces you need to make four coasters and four mugwarmers. You can either follow my designs exactly, or mix and match motifs to create your own.

TO MAKE THE MUGWARMERS

2 For each mugwarmer, cut a piece of calico measuring 8¼ x 3½ in. (21 x 9 cm). Fold it in half widthwise and press, then fold under ⅜ in. (1 cm) on all sides and press again. Cut two 4¾-in. (12-cm) squares of cotton calico for each coaster, fold under ⅜ in. (1 cm) all around, and press.

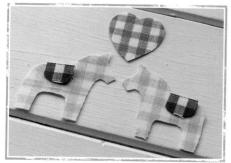

4 Place the pieces on the calico in the right order (a pair of tweezers comes in very handy here). Dab just a tiny bit of glue on the back of the appliqué pieces and press in place.

TO MAKE THE COASTERS

7 Cut out all the appliqué parts from the appropriate colors of gingham. Attach your chosen decorations to one part of each coaster in the same way as for the mugwarmers (see steps 4 and 5). Trim all loose thread ends. Place the decorated coaster on top of an un-decorated patch, both facing right side out. Carefully sew all around the coaster twice, spacing the stitching lines ⅛ in. (2–3 mm) apart.

5 Thread your machine with white thread and sew all the pieces in place; don't forget to open up the mugwarmers so that you don't sew the two sides together by accident.

6 Now it's time to sew the mugwarmers shut. Fold them in half along the central crease, add 10 in. (25 cm) of matching gingham ribbon on either side, and sew all around. Snip the ends of the ribbons into a "V"-shape to make them look extra pretty.

Cafetière COZY

The smell of freshly ground and brewed coffee is one of my absolute favorite fragrances and I could smell it for any length of time! Here I have created a sweet Scandinavian cozy for your cafetière, inspired by the oh so cold Nordic winter mornings, when looking out at the bright blue skies and the crisp and sparkling white snow makes you really appreciate the world for all its beauty.

YOU WILL NEED

- Blue-gray, ocean-blue, and dark gray felt (see steps 1 and 2 for details of how to work out the amounts required)
- Woven ribbon in gray/blue/white, the circumference of your cafetière x 1 in. (25 mm) wide
- Light beige ric-rac braid, twice the circumference of your cafetière x ½ in. (12 mm) wide
- Wooden heart-shaped button, ¾ in. (20 mm) in diameter
- Two ready-made white felt snowflakes 1½ in. (4 cm) in diameter
- Two mother-of-pearl star-shaped buttons, ¾ in. (20 mm) in diameter
- 24 in. (60 cm) each of black and blue gingham ribbon, ⅜ in. (10 mm) wide
- Natural embroidery floss (thread)
- Blue, gray, and white sewing threads
- Basic kit (see page 120)

1 You may not be able to find exactly the same colors that I have used, so lay out all your materials in front of you and make sure the shades go well together. Use pinking shears to cut out two strips of blue-gray felt the circumference of the cafetière just over ⅝ in. (15 mm) deep.

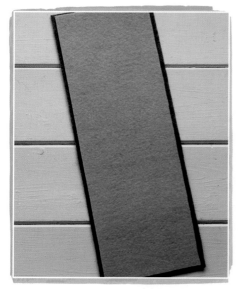

2 Measure the distance between the top and bottom of the handle, minus about ½ in. (1 cm); then measure the circumference of the cafetière, plus about ½ in. (1 cm). Cut a piece of ocean-blue felt to this size. Cut a piece of dark gray felt slightly larger all around than the blue one. Also cut two pieces of blue felt measuring the depth of the large blue strip x 3 in. (8 cm). Lay the gray and small blue pieces to one side for now.

3 Lay the woven ribbon along the center of the blue felt, and stitch it in place with white thread. Lay a thin blue-gray felt strip on either side of the ribbon, with a strip of ric-rac braid on top, and sew along the ric-rac.

4 Stitch the heart-shaped wooden button to the very center of the ribbon, using a matching thread. Using the sewing machine and white thread again, stitch a white felt snowflake on either side of the button, then stitch a star-shaped mother-of-pearl button to the center of each snowflake.

5 Cut the gingham ribbons in half to give two 12-in. (30-cm) lengths of each. Place a blue and a black ribbon together and stitch them to the center of each short side of the gray felt piece, using gray thread.

6 Now you need to cover up all loose ends. Take the two small pieces of blue felt that you cut in step 2 and cut the shorter sides with pinking shears for effect. Fold one piece in half over one short edge of the cozy, so that you have 1½ in. (4 cm) both front and back, and stitch all around with matching sewing thread. Repeat on the other short edge of the cozy.

7 Now place the finished blue patch on top of the gray background piece. Line the two pieces up, making sure the ribbons stick out at the sides. Pin them together and sew all around, using blue as your top thread and gray as your bottom thread.

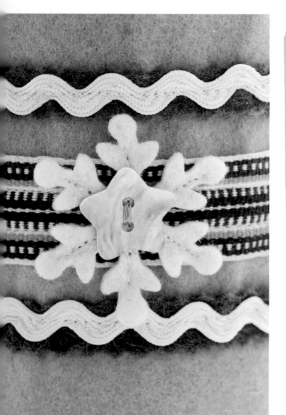

8 Trim all thread ends and stretch the cozy just a little if it has become warped. Wrap the cozy around your cafetière and tie the ribbons in a pretty bow, trimming the ends of the ribbons if they are too long. Now all you have to do is to fill it with steaming hot coffee and get those gorgeous Swedish cinnamon buns out of the oven! (I'll have tea, please!)

TOP TIP

Don't iron the cozy, as synthetic felt melts very easily.

Folklore FLOWER PILLOW

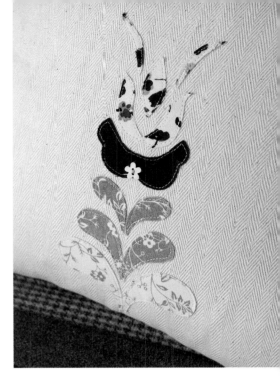

I have completely and utterly fallen in love with a particular type of oven cloth: it is strong, beautifully woven, and has two gorgeous yet simple lines of dark blue running through the fabric. You will see it in several projects in this book. Here I've used it for a wonderfully rustic "kurbits"-inspired pillow case, which will look absolutely fabulous on your summerhouse couch.

YOU WILL NEED

- Templates on page 122
- Two large oven cloths or other sturdy material measuring 30 x 20 in. (75 x 50 cm)
- Scraps of floral, brown, white-on-green, and green-on-white fabrics for the appliqué
- 6-in. (15-cm) square of lightweight iron-on interfacing
- Wooden flower-shaped button, ⅜ in. (10 mm) in diameter
- 60 in. (150 cm) light beige ric-rac braid
- 22 in. (55 cm) beige bias binding
- White sewing thread
- 18-in. (45-cm) square pillow form (cushion pad)
- Basic kit (see page 120)

1 Trace the templates on page 122 onto copy or parchment paper and cut out. Following the manufacturer's instructions, apply iron-on interfacing to the back of the appliqué fabrics to give them a bit of extra strength.

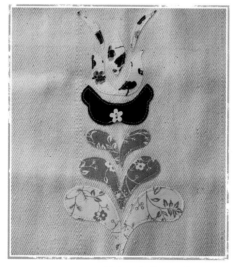

2 Starting 14 in. (35 cm) down from the top edge of one oven cloth and referring to the photo as a guide, machine stitch the six parts of the flower and the leaves in place with white sewing thread. Stitch a wooden flower-shaped button to the center of the brown part.

3 Using a pencil and ruler, draw a dotted line 3 in. (8 cm) in from each long edge of the fabric. Lay the ric-rac braid on top (you can pin it in place if you prefer), and machine stitch it in place, remembering to fold it over the edges at both the top and the bottom for a neater finish.

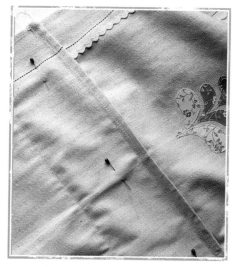

4 Cut the second oven cloth in half. Fold the bias binding to enclose the cut edge of one piece and stitch in place allowing 1 in. (2 cm) or so to stick out at either side for now.

5 Place the full-size oven cloth decorated side down and fold up 5 in. (13 cm) from the bottom edge. If your fabric has lines or a pattern, make sure everything lines up. Place the "half" piece right side up on top, with the bound edge at the top, and pin just these top two layers together along the bottom edge; do not pin through to the decorated front side.

6 Unfold the pillow case, leaving the pins in place. Working from the right side, machine stitch twice across the width, stitching ⅜ in. (1 cm) from the hemmed edge of the half piece and then ⅜ in. (1 cm) from the bottom edge of the decorated piece.

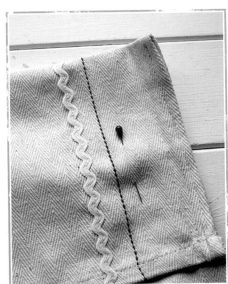

7 Remove the pins and fold up the bottom 5 in. (13 cm) of the pillow case again, decorated side down. Fold 6 in. (15 cm) of the front backward, over the back of the pillow case. Align any lines or patterns, fold in the ends of the bias binding, and pin all three layers together. Sew straight down to the bottom twice on each side, spacing the stitching lines ¼ in. (5 or 6 mm) apart to strengthen the sides.

8 Trim all loose threads, insert the pillow form (cushion pad), and put the pillow on your couch for everyone to adore!

Striped cotton BREAD BASKET

This bread basket is one of my personal favorites—it is so easy to make, and I have made matching ones in various sizes. I love striped material, as do most Scandinavians, and picking a warm and fresh bread bun out of this bag takes me right back to my childhood. As you can see throughout the book, I have a weakness for simple, straight forward motifs and one of my favorites is the bird, which for me symbolizes hopes and dreams—a promise of good days (and breakfasts!) to come.

YOU WILL NEED

- Templates on page 122
- 55 x 14 in. (140 x 35 cm) wide-striped cotton canvas
- Approx. 6-in. (15-cm) square of off-white linen fabric for the appliqué
- Approx. 6-in. (15-cm) square of lightweight iron-on interfacing
- Off-white sewing thread
- Basic kit (see page 120)

1 Cut the striped cotton canvas to the required size—the basket shown here needs a piece 55 in. (140 cm) long x 14 in. (35 cm) wide. If your fabric is not long enough, cut two pieces only half the length and join them together to make a longer one.

2 Press the off-white linen. Following the manufacturer's instructions, apply iron-on interfacing to the back. Trace the templates on page 122 onto copy or parchment paper and cut out. Use the shapes to cut out a bird, a wing, and eight small leaves from the linen.

3 Position the leaves in pairs at the bottom of the bag strip, about 4½ in. (12 cm) from the bottom edge. Dab a little glue onto the back of each leaf to hold it in place while you sew. Thread your sewing machine with off-white sewing thread, then sew all around each leaf in turn and down the middle of each one to create the central "vein." Attach the bird and its wing in the same way.

4 Fold the basket strip in half, with right sides together. Pin and machine stitch around all four sides, taking a ⅜-in. (1-cm) seam allowance and leaving a gap of about 4 in. (10 cm) along the bottom edge.

5 On one bottom corner of the bag, fold the bottom seam up so that it lies over the side seam and forms a triangle. Press and pin in place. Measure 1½ in. (4 cm) up from the tip of the triangle. Using tailor's chalk or a water-soluble fabric marker pen, draw a line across the triangle at this point. Stitch along each line, then cut off the excess fabric with pinking shears. Repeat on the other corners.

6 Turn the basket right side out and close up the little gap by machine—or slipstitch by hand if you prefer.

7 Push in the top part into the bag and wiggle it a bit, to make the bottom square. Fold over 2 in. (5 cm) from the top to finish of your bag. All you have to do now is to put on your apron and get baking!

Nordic VILLAGE SCENE

Funnily enough, my most treasured childhood memories are not of sweets or Christmas presents, as one might imagine, but of the warmth and smell of the hot, dusty gravel roads of my Sweden in summer. In my village they connected nearly every little house and we had a beautiful white church, just like the one in this image. Countless times I ran along these roads with my three sisters, happy for their friendship and company, leaving a cloud of dust behind us.

YOU WILL NEED

- Frame
- Natural-colored thick cotton fabric for the background, at least 3 in. (8 cm) larger than your frame all around
- Dark green leaf-and-berry fabric, 1 in. (2.5 cm) shorter than your frame x 1¼ in. (3 cm) wide
- Scraps of red, white, and green-and-white striped cotton fabric
- Scraps of dark thin leather or imitation leather
- Green, red, white, dark brown, and black sewing threads
- Spray adhesive
- Pair of tweezers
- Small plastic wild boar toy (or a fox, badger, or lynx, if you prefer)—optional
- Superglue
- Basic kit (see page 120)

1 Before you start sewing, you need to mark out how much space you have to play with, since you probably won't be using the very same size of frame as I did. Iron your background material well, place the back of your frame on the fabric, and draw around it, adding ⅜ in. (1 cm) all around. Draw out your design on paper so that you know it'll fit—the shapes are all very simple to draw freehand.

2 Cut a strip of leaf-and-berry fabric slightly shorter than the width of your frame, and fray the top edge a little by pulling off a few strands to give the impression of grass. Stitch the strip in place with green sewing thread. Also cut out a tall pine tree from green-and-white striped material, place it with the trunk just overlapping the grass in the left-hand corner, and attach with green thread.

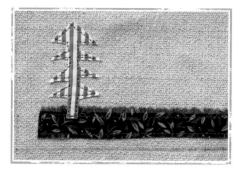

3 Following your drawn design, cut out all the pieces of fabric you need (you can make templates if you want to be really precise, but slight irregularities are part of this project's homespun charm). Cut out a white church and red houses, then stitch them in place with matching sewing thread.

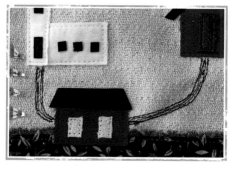

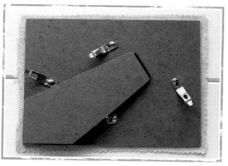

4 Now add the details: cut dark leather roofs for all three buildings, the church door and windows, and a door for one of the houses, and attach each piece of the picture with matching sewing thread. Also cut white windows for the second house out of the background fabric and stitch in place.

5 Using dark brown thread, stitch two parallel lines running between the buildings for the small gravel paths, then stitch in between the two lines to give them a rough texture—just like the real gravel roads of my childhood.

6 Using your pinking shears, cut out the picture along the lines you drew in step 1; it should be just a little bit bigger than your frame. Iron the piece well and place it face down on a flat surface. Carefully spray a thin layer of adhesive over the inside of the back of the frame and place it on the decorated piece. Press it down, then turn it over and smooth out any bubbles; the great thing about spray adhesive is that you have a little bit of time to correct things before it fully sets.

7 Pluck off any loose little threads to finish off the image—a pair of tweezers will come in handy for this.

8 Place your picture in the frame. If you wish, Superglue a wild boar or other forest animal to the inside of the frame to complete your Scandinavian scene!

Fragrant LAVENDER BAGS

Create a sweet keepsake of the magical fragrance of last summer's lavender fields. When the plants are in high bloom, buzzing with bees and butterflies, snip off a few stalks, tie them into a little bundle, and hang them upside down in your window to dry—it should only take a few days. Grab a pretty bowl and pull off all the little purple flowers. These are perfect for winter, when you need a little reminder that the sun really will shine again—soon.

YOU WILL NEED

For one bag

- Approx. 24 x 7 in. (60 x 18 cm) Scandinavian-style striped cotton fabric
- Approx. 10 x 8 in. (25 x 20 cm) white cotton fabric
- 10 in. (25 cm) ribbon
- White sewing thread
- Dried lavender
- Teaspoon
- Basic kit (see page 120)

1 You will need quite a long piece of fabric for each bag—22½ in. (57 cm), to be exact and 7 in. (18 cm) wide. If your chosen material is not long enough, just cut two pieces each measuring 12 in. (30 cm) long, stitch them together to create a longer piece, and press the seam open. Cut across the short ends with pinking shears.

2 With right sides together, aligning the edges, fold the fabric in half and pin together. Machine stitch along the two long outer sides to make a bag. Trim the seam allowances with pinking shears to prevent the fabric from fraying, and snip off the two bottom corners.

3 Turn the bag right side out. Use the tip of a pencil, knitting needle, or wooden skewer to gently push out the bottom corners, taking care not to push right through the fabric. Press well.

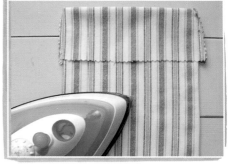

4 Fold over the top 2 in. (5 cm) to create a pretty collar for the bag and press flat again. Leave the bag to one side for now.

5 Now we will make the little lavender pouches that will go
into the larger bags—you need two pouches for each bag.
Press the white cotton fabric and cut four rectangles measuring
4¾ x 3½ in. (12 x 9 cm). Use a quite lightweight cotton fabric,
so that as much of the lovely lavender fragrance can seep out as
possible. Place two pieces on top of each other and pin them
together. Machine stitch around the side and bottom edges, trim
the threads, and snip off the bottom corners. Repeat with the
remaining two rectangles.

6 Turn each pouch right side out. Use the tip of a pencil,
knitting needle, or wooden skewer to push out the bottom
corners, taking care not to push right through the fabric. Press
with a hot iron.

7 Using a teaspoon, fill the pouches
with wonderfully fragrant dried
lavender. Be sure not to fill them too
full or to pack the lavender too hard,
or the fragrance won't have any room
to circulate. Leave about 1–1¼ in.
(2.5–3 cm) of material at the top of each
pouch, since you will need this to close
up the pouches.

8 Fold in the top part of each pouch,
press it flat, and machine stitch across
to close. Trim off the loose threads. Insert
the pouches into the striped bag.

9 Cut a 10-in. (25-cm) length of ribbon
and tie it around the neck of the bag.
Cut a the end of the ribbon on an angle
to finish.

Tasseled HEART TRIO

More often the not, the simplest of decorations are the ones that have the most effect and I find that, when anyone sees these heart decorations in my home, that's what they remember best (except for my excellent cooking skills, of course!).

YOU WILL NEED

- Template on page 122
- One 4-in. (10-cm) square each of red, green, and blue striped fabric
- One 8-in. (20-cm) square of flowery fabric
- Iron-on interfacing (optional)
- Approx. 1 yd (85 cm) natural jute string per decoration
- White sewing thread
- Basic kit (see page 120)

1 Trace the half-heart template on page 122 onto white copy or parchment paper and cut it out. Press the striped and floral fabrics flat. Pin the half-heart template to each fabric in turn and carefully cut out two striped and two floral half-heart shapes for each decoration. Take extra care when cutting the slits for the "fingers"—don't cut them too short, as you can always adjust the length later when you braid (plait) the strips together.

2 Braid (plait) the "fingers" over and under each other, following the instructions for the Braided Half Apron on page 42. Using white thread, carefully sew around the outer edges on your sewing machine. Trim the hearts a little if you need to.

3 To make the tassels, cut five 4-in. (10-cm) lengths of natural jute string and one measuring 14 in. (35 cm). Place four of the short lengths together in a bundle, then wrap the long piece of string around the center of the bundle and tie in a knot, leaving about 12 in. (30 cm) sticking up above the shorter lengths for hanging.

TOP TIP

If your chosen material is too flimsy, back it first with iron-on interfacing before you cut out the parts.

4 Fold the two sets of short strings for the tassel down below the knot, then tie the fifth short length of string around the tassel just below the first knot to hold everything in place. Trim all the tassel strings to the same length.

5 Work out where on the long jute string you want to position the heart, then place the string in the very center of the back of one heart part, making sure it lies straight. Place the second heart on top of the first one and line all parts up carefully. Take your time and sew all around the braided heart, checking frequently to make sure that the string is still where it's supposed to be!

6 At the top of the long jute string, tie a loop for hanging the heart later. Repeat steps 1–6 to make the remaining hearts. I hung my hearts at three different heights on their strings for a staggered effect, but you can of course attach yours how you wish.

Braided COTTON RUG

I chose green and natural white colors for this rug because of my weakness for the "Gustavian" palette, which was developed by the Swedish aristocracy during the 17th and 18th centuries. It was inspired by the extravaganza of Italian, French, and British courts at the time, but Scandinavians—as always, proclaiming that less is more—toned it down considerably and created this distinctive and immediately recognizable look. It also makes a lovely soft floor covering for a child's bedroom.

YOU WILL NEED

- 2¾ yd (2.4 m) each of two co-ordinating cotton fabrics. 44 in. (112 cm) wide
- White sewing thread
- Strong sewing machine needle—size 90
- Basic kit (see page 120)

Basic kit (see page 120)

TOP TIP

Make sure you have a strong sewing machine needle or it might break.

1 I chose two co-ordinating fabrics—one with a white pattern on a pale green background, the other with a pale green pattern on white—that complement each other perfectly. Cut your fabric horizontally into six strips 16 in. (40 cm) deep, then cut each of those strips vertically into strips 2 in. (5 cm) wide. You will end up with 132 strips of each fabric, to make 44 braids in all.

2 Lay three strips on top of each other: the top and bottom strips should be in the same fabric, and the middle strip in the contrasting fabric. Sew across the tops and cut clean with pinking shears.

3 If you happen to have a friend or family member at home, ask them to hold the end for you while you braid (plait); otherwise, sit on the floor, tuck the end in under your heel, and braid away to your heart's content. Sew the ends together as before. Make up 44 braids in the same way.

4 Place three braids very close together and stitch across the middle to join them together. They might come slightly apart, but don't worry, as you will be going over the same patch later. Add the next three braids in the same way. Continue doing this until you have used up all the braids.

5 When you get to the end, turn the rug and sew again along the path you came, pressing the braids tightly together as you sew. Working outward from the center seam, sew lines about 1¼ in. (3 cm) apart until you have secured all the braids all the way out to the edges. If any of the braids are too long, just sew line of stitching across it, then cut off the excess with pinking shears.

Vintage dish-towel
DOILY PILLOW

If you never have visited a bustling Scandinavian flea market, you absolutely must! You never know what you might find—and since we Northerners treasure our heritage so much, you have an ocean of vintage and well-loved paraphernalia, which will look fab in your modern home. Growing up in Sweden, I always bought hand-crocheted cotton doilies and vintage dish towels. I've put them to good use in making this pillow!

YOU WILL NEED

- Two vintage dish towels
- Selection of large and small white crocheted cotton doilies
- 48 in. (120 cm) gingham ribbon, 2.5 in. (1 cm) wide, to match the dish towels
- Polyester toy filling
- White sewing thread
- Wooden spoon
- Basic kit (see page 120)

1 For this project, select two dish towels that have the same grid pattern, so that you can line them up precisely. Measure 14 in. (35 cm) from the top edge down on one of the dish towels and set a pin there; this marks the bottom edge of the front of the cover and you now know how much space you have to play with. Lay out clean and ironed small and large cotton doilies in your chosen pattern and pin in place.

2 Using white sewing thread, machine stitch the doilies in place—but leave the outer "leaves" or points loose, so that the cover looks a little more alive.

3 Cut the gingham ribbon into four equal lengths. Machine stitch two lengths to the top of each dish towel, 2 in. (5 cm) in from the side edges.

4 Place the decorated dish towel on top of the plain one and pin together. At 14 in. (35 cm) down (the point you marked with a pin in step 1), cut a straight line across both layers with pinking shears to prevent the fabric from fraying.

5 Pin the two dish towels right sides together and machine stitch along the side and bottom edges, leaving the top edge open for now. Snip off the tips of the bottom corners for a neater finish. Turn the cover right side out and carefully push out the corners with the handle of your wooden spoon. Press the cover, and check that everything is straight and even.

6 Fill the cover with toy filling and pin the two layers together along the top edge. Sew along the top, making sure that the ribbons on the front and back of the cover align.

7 Finally, tie the ribbons in a bow and snip the ends of each ribbon into a "V-shape" for an extra-pretty finish. Plump up the pillow and it's ready to decorate your home!

Kurbits-style DOORSTOP

Sweden has a long and very rich tradition of folk-art painting that translates beautifully to textiles—particularly to appliqué work. I've based this design on "kurbits" painting, a style that flourished between the mid-18th and mid-19th centuries in the province of Dalarna and southern Norrland and is still practiced today to create wonderful craft items such as the famed Dala horse. It features very stylized flowers and leaves, and wonderful bright colors. Here is my interpretation—a practical but very decorative doorstop for your home. I've added a genuine Sami ribbon, which I was lucky enough to have in my stash, but any bright woven ribbon would work.

MATERIAL

- Templates on page 122
- Approx. ¼ yd (20 cm) thick striped cotton material, 36 in. (90 cm) wide
- Scraps of red, blue, and mustard-yellow felt
- Red, white, blue, and yellow round beads, 3 mm in diameter
- Approx. 7 oz (200 g) dried beans or rice
- Polyester toy filling
- Woven Sami ribbon, approx. 8 x 1 in. (20 x 2.5 cm)—a bookmark works well, too
- Red, blue, mustard-yellow, and white sewing threads
- Wooden spoon
- Basic kit (see page 120)

1 Cut out five 6¾-in. (17-cm) squares of sturdy striped cotton fabric. The doorstop will look best if you cut the patches looking exactly the same with all the stripes lining up. On four of the patches, draw a triangle on the back: the top of the triangle should be in the very center of the top edge, 3⅜ in. (8.5 cm) from each side. Using pinking shears, cut out all four triangles.

2 Trace the templates on page 122 onto white copy or parchment paper and cut out. Use to cut out the flower base in red felt, the petals in blue felt, and the center of the flower in mustard yellow felt.

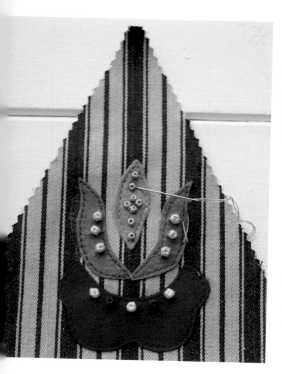

3 Starting with the red flower base so that you know where to place the rest of the decorations, and using matching threads, stitch all the flower parts to the right side of one of the triangles. Attach pretty little beads to the felt decoration: red and white to the red flower base, blue to the blue petals, and tiny yellow ones to the flower center.

4 With right sides together, aligning the straight base with one side of the square, pin and stitch one triangle to the square base patch. Repeat with the remaining three triangles. Press the seams open.

5 This step might seem tricky, but it really isn't: lay two adjoining triangle sides on top of each other, with right sides together. Pin and sew. Pin and stitch the remaining sides in the same way, but leave a 2-in. (5-cm) gap in the last side.

6 Turn the pyramid right side out through the gap and gently push out the four corners with the handle of a wooden spoon. Fill your doorstop with about 7 oz (200 g) of dried beans or rice.

7 Add a bit of bulk to the pyramid by filling the remaining space with toy filling. Make sure you add enough to expand it fully.

8 Fold in the seam allowance on either side of the gap and slipstitch (see page 121) the gap closed. Give the door stopper a few squeezes and pats, to make sure all seams are fully closed and it holds the shape well.

9 Attach the Sami ribbon to the tip of the pyramid by hand, using small stitches in a matching color of thread. And there you have it—a gorgeous and very Scandinavian doorstop!

Nordic FOLKLORE BUNTING

Every home should have a bit of bunting! It "dresses" a room straight away and cheers you up every time it catches your eye. I have used very soft natural shades and added just a little bit of color in the decorations for a smooth, Scandinavian look—but feel free to spice it up a little if you prefer.

YOU WILL NEED

- Templates on page 122
- 11 x 9 in. (28 x 23 cm) each of three natural-colored cotton fabrics in different shades
- 7-in. (18-cm) square of vintage floral fabric

- Scraps of pale green-and-white floral fabric
- 32 x 20 in. (80 x 50 cm) lightweight iron-on interfacing
- 65 in. (165 cm) cream ric-rac braid

- Natural, white, and green sewing threads
- Flat-backed pink and green flower gems (optional)
- PVA glue (optional)
- Basic kit (see page 120)

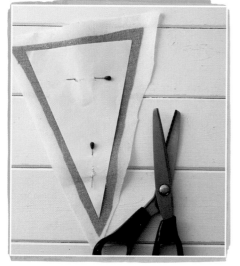

1 Trace the templates on page 122 onto copy or parchment paper and cut out. Cut out two large triangles of each natural-colored cotton fabric and apply lightweight iron-on interfacing to the back. Pin the triangle template onto each large triangle in turn, then cut around it with pinking shears.

2 Apply iron-on interfacing to the backs of all the appliqué fabrics. For the flower bunting, use the darkest of your natural-colored fabrics as the flag. Using the template on page 122, draw two circles on the back of the floral fabric, then cut them out with pinking shears or scallop-edged craft scissors. Using white sewing thread, machine stitch one flower head to each dark triangle.

3 Cut out two small white leaves and two large green ones, remembering to flip the templates so that you get two reversed leaves. Stitch on the two small leaves and then the large ones just below the flower. From the remnants, cut four little oval leaves from the white fabric and two from the green and add them as shown.

4 Using matching green thread, machine stitch a straight line down from where the two large leaves meet to 2 in. (5 cm) from the bottom tip. Turn around and sew back up again, and then down again, to make the stem fuller.

5 Using the templates, cut out two Dala horses and birds from floral fabric, and two saddles and wings from green fabric. (Remember to flip the template over before you cut out the second of each shape.) Attach the Dala horses and saddles to the palest of your chosen background fabrics, and the birds to the medium shade, using white sewing thread.

6 Lay the bunting flags out in front of you, with the two Dala horses in the middle, then the birds, and finally the flowers. The horses' and birds' head should be pointing in toward the center.

7 Decide how much ric-rac you want to leave to hang the bunting, then pin the flags face down to the ric-rac in the correct order. Machine stitch them in place, using shades of thread to match your fabrics. If you wish, glue a little flat-backed gem to the ric-rac in between each bunting flag as an extra decoration.

Braided HALF APRON

Mmmm, the smells from the kitchen when I was a child in Sweden were mouth-watering! Both of my grandmothers and my mother were fantastic chefs; they could create flavors and textures that I have not tasted anywhere else since. All three of them are gone from us now, and I try my best to re-create the fabulous food they placed in front of me and my three sisters for my own children. I am not sure how close I get, though! This apron, with its strong, sturdy material and braided Scandinavian heart, is my small way of saying thank you.

MATERIAL

- Template on page 122
- ¾ yd (70 cm) thick natural or light beige cotton canvas, 44 in. (112 cm) wide
- Approx. 6-in. (15-cm) square of red cotton material
- Approx. 6-in. (15-cm) square of small-checked red-and-white gingham
- Approx. 6 in. (15 cm) iron-on lightweight interfacing
- Approx. 6 in. (15 cm) fusible bonding web
- Light beige crocheted cotton doily, 12 in. (30 cm) in diameter
- 60 in. (150 cm) natural or light beige ric-rac braid
- Three wooden heart-shaped buttons approx. ½ in. (12 mm) tall
- Natural or light beige sewing thread
- Red embroidery floss (thread)
- Spray adhesive
- Basic kit (see page 120)

TOP TIP

If your doily is second hand, wash it first and press it flat. Check for any loose ends that might unravel, and mend these. If your doily is new, make sure it is colorfast, so that it won't end up staining the apron.

1 Cut a rectangle of cotton canvas measuring approx. 20 x 27 in. (50 x 70 cm). Turn under ⅜ in. (1 cm) to the wrong side around all four sides. Press and pin in place. Using matching sewing thread, machine stitch around all four sides to prevent fraying. It will be a bumpy ride, since the material is so thick, but just take it slowly and be careful not to break the needle.

2 Trace the half-heart template on page 122 onto white copy paper or parchment paper and cut it out. Press the gingham and red cotton fabrics flat. Following the manufacturer's instructions, apply iron-on interfacing to the back of each fabric.

3 Pin the half-heart template onto each fabric in turn and carefully cut out one piece of each. Take extra care when cutting the slits for the "fingers"—don't cut them too short, as you can always adjust the length later when you braid (plait) the strips together.

4 Place the red half-heart on top of the gingham heart and braid (plait) the "fingers" over and under each other, as shown, so that you get alternate squares; start by lifting the left-hand red finger over the right-hand gingham finger, then take it under the middle gingham finger and over the left-hand gingham finger. The next finger has to go the opposite way and the last finger will need to be braided like the first one. To complete the heart, pull it gently on all sides, so that it all slips into place, then trim off any edges that stick out a little longer than the others.

5 Lay out your apron flat in front of you (iron it first if necessary) and mark the very center with a tiny pencil dot. Spray the back of the doily with adhesive (spray adhesive is a fantastic invention—it doesn't smear or run and you can easily take off the item if it's not positioned right), then place your doily in the center of the apron, using the pencil dot as a guide.

6 Since the doily will hang on the apron, so to speak, you need to make sure that it stays flat. Using pins and following the circular pattern, mark four concentric circles around the doily that you can sew around. Using a sewing thread as close in color to the doily as possible, and starting in the center, sew around the first circle, then space out another two circles. Finally, sew all along the very top points of the doily, trying to make sure it doesn't get pushed askew. The best way to test if you have sewn enough is to simply hold up the apron in the air and check that the doily holds firm.

7 Following the manufacturer's instructions, apply fusible bonding web to the back of the heart and apply it the center of the doily. Using matching thread, machine stitch all around the heart to attach it firmly to the apron. To make sure that the "fingers" don't ravel, sew along the edges of each one.

TOP TIP

I find that it is very helpful to add just a dab of glue on the fingers that lie on the top of the heart, to keep them in place as you sew. Then flip the heart over and do the same on the reverse.

8 To decorate the apron further, cut two 30-in. (75-cm) lengths of ric-rac braid: they need to be just a little longer than the width of the apron, so that you can fold them under at the sides. Using a pencil or a fade-away fabric marker, draw a series of small lines across the top and cotton of the apron, about 1¼ in. (3 cm) from the edge. Pin the ric-rac along this line, folding the excess over to the back of the apron, then machine stitch in place.

9 Now we are nearly done with the apron—only the pocket and straps left! For the pocket, cut a small rectangle of the same material as your apron, measuring 4¾ x 5½ in. (12 x 14 cm). Fold under ⅜ in. (1 cm) all the way around and press.

10 Trace the leaf template on page 122 onto copy or parchment paper and cut out. From the interfaced gingham left over from the heart, cut out four small leaves. Pin them to the lower part of the pocket and stitch in place. Pin the pocket to the upper left-hand side of the apron as you look at it, then sew around the sides and base edges twice, to secure it well. (If you are left handed, place the pocket on the right-hand side of the apron.) Thread a needle with red embroidery floss (thread) and attach a little wooden heart-shaped button to the top of the pocket.

11 The last thing we need to make are the straps. Cut four lengths of apron material measuring 27 x 3½ in. (70 x 9 cm). Fold in ⅜ in. (1 cm) along each long side and press flat; keep checking as you go along that the fold is even all the way along. Place two straps on top of each other, right sides out, and pin together. Machine stitch along both long edges, just inside the edge, but do not stitch the short ends just yet.

12 Fold in ⅜ in. (1 cm) on one short end of each strap and press flat. Place that end of each strap on the upper part of the back of the apron, about 2 in. (5 cm) from the edge, and box stitch (see page 121) in place.

13 Turn in the bottom ends of the straps as before, press flat, and box stitch. Using red embroidery floss (thread) again, stitch a heart-shaped button to the center of each of the squares.

Dala horse DIARY

For me, there is nothing better than a brand new notebook filled with lined or with blank white pages—to open it for the first time and smell the paper is so lovely! In winter time when it's cold outside, it's nice to sit and pen some plans for spring or maybe reminisce about seasons gone. But the outside of a notebook is often not very pretty and doesn't reflect you as a person, so here's how make your very own Scandinavian winter scene that will cozy-up your notebook, for sure. Originally from Sweden, the Dala horse has, over the centuries, become a symbol of the North; for us, it is a sign of regional pride and togetherness, and gives us a sense of belonging.

MATERIAL

- Hardcover notebook
- Templates on page 123
- Pebble gray felt (see step 1)
- Scraps of red and white felt
- Red and white sewing threads
- Basic kit (see page 120)

1 Start by measuring the height and width of your notebook (there are many different sizes). If you lay the book flat on its back, holding all the pages between your fingers in the air, and measure straight down the back and across the sides of the book, you really can't go wrong. Write down your measurements and add about ½ in. (1 cm) all around, to give yourself just that little bit of room later. Cut a piece of pebble gray felt to this size.

2 Trace the Dala horse, heart, and snowflake templates on page 123 onto copy or parchment paper, and cut them out. Then pin the horse template onto red felt and cut out one horse shape.

3 Using the templates, cut out one heart from red felt and one snowflake from white felt. Also cut a length of white felt almost the width of the front cover of your notebook and about ½ in. (1 cm) high, cutting one long edge with pinking shears and the others with straight scissors; this is to symbolize the snow.

TOP TIP

If you are worried that the motifs might move while you're stitching them, apply a line of glue to the back first.

4 Fold the cover piece in half and mark the middle with a large pin—this way you will know exactly how much room you have to decorate. Using the photo as a guide, place the snow at the bottom, then the horse, and finally the snowflake with the little red heart, gleaming over it all. When you're happy with the positions, machine stitch the snow in place, using white thread to match the felt.

5 Cut a tiny semicircle of white felt freehand for the saddle. Glue the top edge only to the back of the horse—let the rest of the saddle hang loose. Still using white thread, sew all around the Dala horse. Take it slowly and stop and check where you are often—white thread on a red background can really show up any mistakes. Sew the reins and bridle in white thread, too, then lift up the saddle and stitch the girth.

6 Place the white felt snowflake above the Dala horse. Load your sewing machine with red thread and sew three straight separate lines across the snowflake to attach it to the felt, making sure that the lines cross in the middle. Change your thread to white again, place the red heart in the center of the snowflake, and stitch it in place. There we go—a lovely Scandinavian winter scene in no time.

7 Now it's time to assemble the cover. Cut two inner side panels as tall as the book cover and 2½ in. (6 cm) wide. Turn the cover wrong side up, and pin one side panel to each short edge. Using white thread, sew all around the cover about ⅛ in. (3 mm) from the edge.

8 Insert your notebook—it might be a little tight at first, but the felt will shape itself around the notebook. Close over the notebook and smooth it out—make sure the edges are straight. Now all there is left to do is to open the very first page and start writing down your thoughts and memories!

Appliquéd KEY FOB

This sweet appliquéd key fob carries all the hallmarks of traditional Scandinavian style—a sleek design, clean lines, and, of course, a bit of wood! I created it out of pure desperation, since I can never find my keys when I need them... and so this slightly retro key fob was born! It is so simple to make—why not make some to give as presents, too?

YOU WILL NEED

- 11 x 3 in. (28 x 8 cm) thick, neutral-colored cotton canvas or calico
- Scraps of striped or checkered fabric for the leaves
- Scraps of lightweight iron-on interfacing
- 4 in. (10 cm) brown ribbon, ⅜ in. (10 mm) wide
- Wooden heart button, approx. ½ in. (12 mm) in diameter
- Medium gray and neutral/light beige sewing threads
- Metal key ring
- Pencil, knitting needle, or wooden skewer
- Basic kit (see page 120)

1 Cut two rectangles of thick, durable cotton canvas or calico measuring 5½ x 3 in. (14 x 8 cm); these measurements include a ⅜-in. (1-cm) seam allowance. Cut the short ends using pinking shears, to keep the patches from fraying.

TOP TIP

You can either cut the leaves freehand or use the template for the Braided Half Apron on page 122.

2 Pick three fabrics for the leaves. Pale, striped fabrics are a sure favorite in Scandinavia, but using a checkered fabric helps to break it up a little. Following the manufacturer's instructions, apply iron-on interfacing to the backs of the fabrics and cut out a pair of leaf shapes from each fabric. Lay the leaves out in pairs on one piece of fabric. We will attach a little wooden button later; include this in your layout, to make sure you leave room for it at the top.

3 Dab a little glue on the back of each of the leaves before you start sewing—they are very keen on moving around, for some reason! Thread your sewing machine with medium-gray sewing thread. Sew all around each leaf in turn, then sew down the middle of each one to create the central "vein." Sew a "stem" connecting all the leaves, continuing up a little way beyond the leaves so that there is something to attach "the flower" (the wooden button) to later.

4 Place the front patch right side down on top of the back patch, lining up the edges carefully, and pin together at the bottom. Fold your length of ribbon in half to make a loop. Place it at the top of the patch, with the loop pointing inward, and pin it in place. Sew all along the sides and top with neutral or light beige sewing thread, leaving the bottom edge open. You might want to go forth and back over the ribbon a few times, to make sure it's firmly secured.

5 Cut around the stitched sides with pinking shears, to keep the material from fraying, and snip off the upper corners.

6 Turn the patch right side out and check the seams to make sure there are no gaps. If there are, just turn it wrong side out again and sew a little more where needed; it's no fun to discover this after you have completed the patch! Use the tip of a pencil, knitting needle, or wooden skewer to push out the upper corners, taking care not to push right through the fabric. Press with a hot iron.

7 Fold in the raw edges at the bottom of the patch and press in place. Sew all around the entire patch, just inside the edge. This is a bumpy ride, especially if you use very thick cotton canvas as I did, but take your time—one stitch at a time and you'll do fine!

8 Using a thread close to the button color, stitch the button to the top of the "stem," making sure you don't stitch through to the back of the patch. Press again if necessary. Attach a metal key ring to the ribbon loop.

Scandi LAPTOP COVER

There are plenty of mass-produced gadget sleeves and covers to be had, but who wants to be like everyone else? Here's an eye-catching cover for your laptop, lined with super-soft batting (wadding) to keep it safe. Made from sturdy, natural cotton canvas, it's embellished with a very Nordic-looking appliqué motif in crisp blue and white fabrics. My cotton canvas has a thin blue line 2 in. (5 cm) from the top and bottom, which complements the appliqué—but if your material doesn't have that, you could add it with simple backstitch.

1 First, work out how much fabric you need. Laptops come in different sizes and thicknesses, so measure the length and depth of your laptop, and add these two figures together. Then measure the height and depth of your laptop, and add these two figures together. Add 1½ in. (4 cm) all around to allow for the seam allowances, then cut two pieces of cotton canvas to this size.

YOU WILL NEED

- Templates on page 122
- Thick natural or light beige cotton canvas (see step 1)
- Natural/light beige crocheted cotton doily 12 in. (30cm) in diameter
- Blue-and-white striped and chequered cotton fabrics for the appliquéd heart
- Lightweight iron-on interfacing
- Thick 4-oz (100-g) batting (wadding)
- Light beige ric-rac braid
- 6-in. (15-cm) length of brown- and-beige polka-dot ribbon
- Beige bias binding
- Wooden heart button, ½ in. (12 mm) tall
- Natural/light beige sewing thread
- Light beige embroidery floss (thread)
- Spray adhesive
- Basic kit (see page 120)

2 Cut a length of light beige ric-rac braid about 1 in. (2–3 cm or so) longer than one long edge of the cotton canvas for the front cover. Using a pencil and ruler, draw a dotted line along the bottom edge 1¼ in. (3 cm) from the edge. Place the ric-rac on the line (you can pin it in place if you prefer), tuck the raw ends under, and stitch in place.

3 Lay the front cover out vertically in front of you (iron it flat first if necessary). At the bottom of the cover, just above the ric-rac line and centered widthwise, spray on a circle of adhesive slightly smaller than the diameter of your doily. Press your doily down firmly to make it all stick together.

TIP

Be careful not to apply too much spray adhesive—any excess liquid will leave dark and hard marks on the material.

4 Using pins and following the circular pattern of the doily, mark four concentric circles around the doily that you can sew around. Using a sewing thread as close in color to the doily as possible, and starting in the center, sew around the first circle, then space out another two circles. Finally, sew all along the very top points of the doily, trying to make sure it doesn't get pushed askew as you stitch.

5 Trace the half-heart template on page 122 onto white copy paper or parchment paper and cut it out. Press the striped and checkered fabrics flat. Following the manufacturer's instructions, apply iron-on interfacing to the back of each fabric.

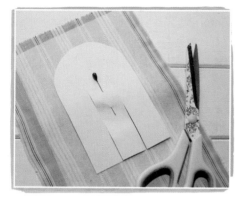

6 Pin the half-heart template onto each fabric in turn and carefully cut out one piece of each. Take extra care when cutting the slits for the "fingers"—don't cut them too short, as you can always adjust the length later.

7 Braid (plait) the "fingers" over and under each other, following the instructions for the Braided Half Apron on page 42. Place the heart in the very center of the doily and secure it temporarily with a tiny amount of spray adhesive. Sew all around the heart to secure it. Also sew along both sides of each "finger," to keep them from moving around.

8 Finally, trace the leaf template on page 122 onto white copy paper or parchment paper and cut it out. Use to cut eight little leaves from the leftover interfaced fabrics; you need four of each fabric. Place them just underneath the heart and sew them in place individually, stitching all the way around and then down the middle of each one to create a central "vein."

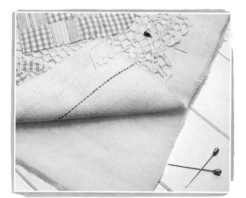

9 Place the front laptop cover piece on thick batting (wadding), pin the layers together, and cut the batting to size. Machine stitch around all four sides about ⅜ in. (1 cm) from the edge to secure the batting to the cover piece. Repeat with the back cover.

10 Cut a length of beige bias binding about 2 in. (5 cm) longer than the top edge of the front cover. Pin it right side down to the batting (wadding) and carefully sew all along the top crease. Repeat on the back cover.

11 Fold the bias binding over to the front of the cover piece, pin it in place, and topstitch along the edge; it will be a bit of a tight squeeze to enclose both the batting (wadding) and the canvas inside the binding, but be patient and take your time. Repeat on the back cover.

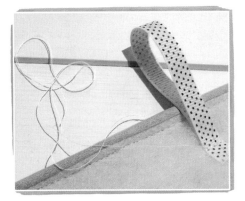

12 Cut a 6-in. (15-cm) length of brown-and-beige polka-dot ribbon. Mark the very middle of the upper part of the back cover. Fold the ribbon in half to make a loop and pin it in place. Using light beige sewing thread, stitch over the loose ends of the loop a few times to secure it in place.

TIPS

If you have any lines on your material, like I did, make sure to match up the lines on the front and back before you pin the layers together.

Use long pins: you're going through four layers, so the cover will be very thick.

Most likely your sewing-machine foot will get caught in the wadding, so keep a sharp pair of scissors at hand to snip it free.

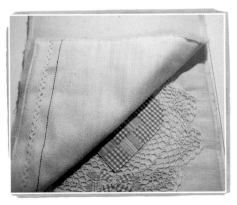

13 Pin the two cover pieces right sides together. Sewing just inside the seam that attaches the batting (wadding) to the canvas, sew around the bottom and side edges. When you've finished, place your laptop in the inside-out cover to make sure it sits snugly; if the cover is too loose, just stitch another seam to make it a tighter fit.

14 Finally, to really give the laptop cover that rustic northern look, add a small wooden button to the top of the front cover, just where the loop will close over it. There are plenty of button shapes to choose from out there, but I love the heart-shaped ones!

Lingonberry BAG

Before I made my first ever bag, it felt like such an obstacle to learn how to sew one—but it really is so simple. Have a try and I can promise you that you will soon be making more! With this particular bag, I pay homage to my home country of Sweden by adding the proud Dala horse and one of the most delicious finds in our forests—the lingonberry. If you've never tried one before, it's a bit like a cranberry—but I think it's sweeter and even more tasty!

YOU WILL NEED

- Templates on page 123
- 21½ in. (55 cm) strong natural cotton canvas, 60 in. (150 cm) wide, for the outer bag and straps; alternatively, use two industrial oven cloths
- 31½ x 21½ in. (80 x 55 cm) large red-and-white polka-dot fabric for the lining
- 10-in. (25-cm) square of large red-and-white polka-dot fabric for the strap centers
- 8-in. (20-cm) square of dark green lingonberry or leaf-and-berry fabric for the Dala horse appliqué
- Scraps of striped, small polka-dot, and large polka-dot in green/white and red/white, plus tiny scraps of solid red, for the leaf and berry appliqués
- Approx. 66 in. (165 cm) red-and-white striped ribbon, ⅜ in. (1 cm) wide
- Red and white sewing threads
- Wooden spoon
- Basic kit (see page 120)

1 Trace the templates on page 123 onto white copy or parchment paper and cut them out. Use to cut out the appliqué pieces—the Dala horse from the lingonberry fabric, the saddle from red-and-white striped fabric, the large berry and leaves from the large polka-dot fabrics, and the small berries and leaves from the small polka-dot and striped fabrics.

2 For the bag, cut a piece of cotton canvas measuring 21½ x 31½ in. (55 x 80 cm); alternatively, use an industrial oven cloth. Fold it in half widthwise and press a crease along the bottom edge, so that you can see where the bottom of the bag will be. Open out the fabric again, then lay out the design, making sure it all fits.

TOP TIP

If you are using cut material, start by folding and sewing a ⅜-in. (1-cm) hem at the top and bottom of your material. Industrial oven cloths tend to have that already done.

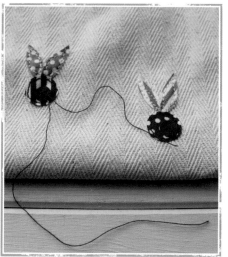

3 Thread your machine with white sewing thread and sew on the horse and its saddle. Then add the large leaves and lingonberry.

4 Along the lower edge of the bag, add the small lingonberries—you can add as many or as few as you wish. Alternate the fabrics—striped lingonberry with dotted leaves and dotted lingonberry with striped leaves. Also add a tiny circle of solid red fabric to each berry, attaching it with just a few small hand stitches. Use white thread for the leaves and red for the berries.

5 To frame the Scandinavian setting, add a line of lovely red-and-white striped ribbon. I find it a lot easier to sew if I have previously drawn a dotted line to guide me, as it is very easy to stray off course when you are concentrating on the machine. Let ½ in. (1 cm or so) stick out at each end. Lay your bag fabric flat and attach the ribbon by stitching along each long edge of the ribbon.

6 Iron the red-and-white large polka-dot lining material. Fold over ⅜ in. (1 cm) to the wrong side along the top and bottom edges and press. With wrong sides together, pin the lining material to the back of the bag along the top and bottom edges. Sew along the top and bottom edges, folding the ribbon ends in under the lining fabric as you sew.

7 To make the straps, cut four strips of strong cotton canvas (or use a second industrial oven cloth), each measuring 3 x 27½ in. (7.5 x 70 cm). Lay two strips on top of each other, right sides together, and sew along three sides, leaving one short edge open. Trim all threads and turn the strap right side out. (The handle of a wooden spoon will come in handy for this!) Repeat to make the second strap. Press the straps well and turn in the open ends.

8 Fold each strap in half and press. Measure 4½ in. (11.5 cm) out from the center crease in each direction and mark with a pin.

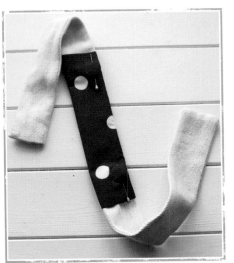

9 Cut two pieces of the large red-and-white large polka-dot lining material, each measuring 5 x 10 in. (12.5 x 25 cm). Press under ⅜ in. (1 cm) to the wrong side on all four sides. Wrap one piece around each of the straps, between the pins you inserted in the previous step, and pin in place. Carefully sew all around the strap, as close to the edge as possible, to join the layers together.

10 On the right side of the front of the bag, place one end of the first strap 2 in. (5 cm) down from the upper edge and 3½ in. (9 cm) in from the side edge and box stitch in place (see page 121). Sew twice around the box, to make sure is securely fastened. Do the same on the other side of the front, then repeat on the right side of the back of the bag with the second strap. Turn the bag inside out and sew along the side edges to complete.

11 Trim all loose thread ends and turn your bag right side out. Gently push out the corners with the handle of your wooden spoon.

Dala horse EARPHONE TIDY

The Dala horse is said by some people of be a model of Sleipnir, the god Odin's eight-legged horse, who carried the bravely fallen warriors to Valhalla. Originally carved as a toy for children, it has become a symbol of the province of Dalarna, and of Sweden in general. This project combines ancient history with modern technology, creating a colorful holder for your high-tech earphones! Decorated with gorgeous traditional Scandinavian ribbons and light embroidery, it is the perfect combination of old and new.

YOU WILL NEED

- Template on page 123
- 5-in. (12-cm) square each of red and white felt
- 4 in. (10 cm) Scandinavian patterned ribbon, ¼ in. (7 mm) wide
- Red, green, and yellow embroidery flosses (threads)
- Green and white sewing threads
- Basic kit (see page 120)

1 Trace the template on page 123 onto white copy or parchment paper and cut it out. Pin the template to white felt and cut out two shapes, then cut two more horses from red felt.

2 I found a fabulous red, green, and yellow ribbon with Scandinavian details in my stash and it is perfect for this project. Cut two 2-in. (5-cm) lengths of ribbon; this is a little bit longer than you need for the girth and reins, since we will fold them in at the back later. Load your sewing machine with green thread and carefully stitch the ribbons to the white front of the horse.

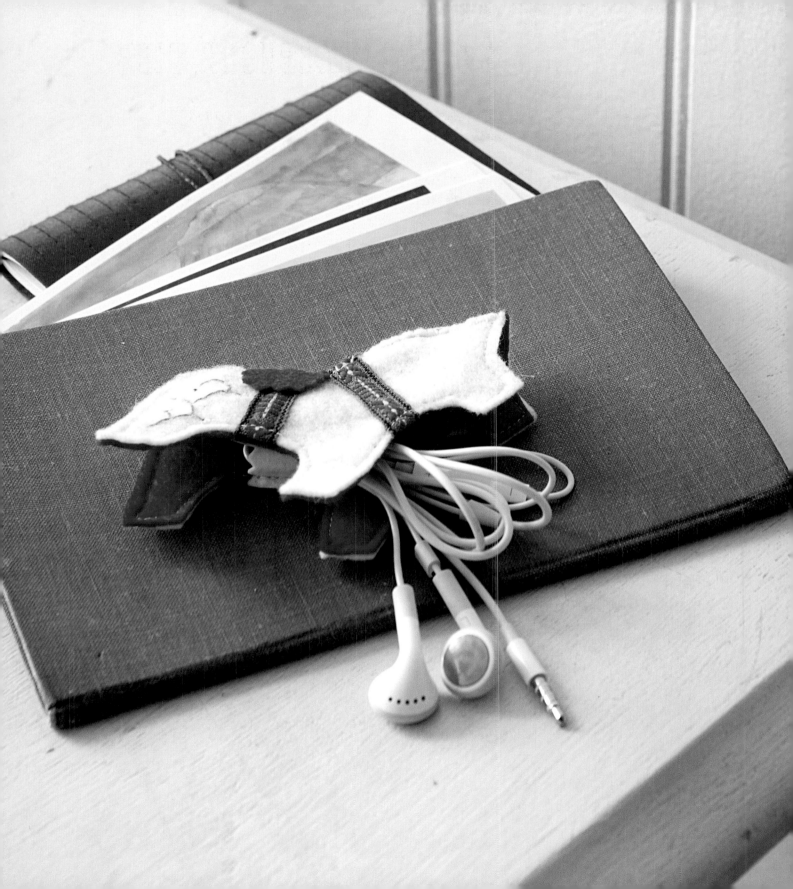

3 Decorate the horse's back leg by embroidering a bit of greenery using backstitch, tiny yellow flowers in straight stitch, and red French knots for the flower centers. They are very easy to sew freehand and make the horse look so lovely. I used two strands of floss (thread).

4 Using pinking shears around the curved edge, cut a small semicircle of red felt for the saddle. Place the decorated white horse on one of the red horses, folding the ends of the ribbons in between the two layers, and position the saddle in place; you can pin the layers together if you wish. Load your sewing machine with white thread and carefully stitch all around the horse. Trim around the edges if any of the red felt shows on the white side.

5 Using pinking shears, cut a 2 x ⅜-in. (5 x 1-cm) strip of white felt to hold the earphones. Using white thread, stitch the top and bottom edges of the white strip to the remaining red horse, in line with the girth on the decorated horse. Now, place the red horse on the white undecorated horse and carefully sew them together on your machine, using white thread.

6 Use a sharp needle and white thread (or you have no chance of getting through four layers of felt), blanket stitch (see page 121) the front and back horse together, sewing from the left edge of the saddle to the top left of the ear.

7 Wind your earphones together and insert them into the white loop. Perfect! There we go, another problem solved. Your little Dala horse will take great care of your earphones—and you must agree, it looks quite stylish, too!

Cool blue iPAD COVER

Many of us take our iPads or tablets everywhere we go and constantly pulling them in and out of your bag can easily result in the surface getting scratched and damaged. Here I have made a cheery light blue and very sweet cover, to help protect your favorite gadget Nordic style! I made mine for a iPad, but you can adapt the measurements to fit whatever gadget you choose (see step 1).

YOU WILL NEED

- Templates on page 123
- 36 x 45 in. (90 x 115 cm) light blue felt
- 4¾ x 4¾ in. (12 x 12 cm) light pink felt
- Scraps of red and green felt
- 20 in. (50 cm) red bias binding
- Light blue and pink round beads, 3 mm in diameter
- Light blue and pink embroidery floss (thread)
- Red, light pink, and green sewing threads
- Fabric glue
- Basic kit (see page 120)

1 First measure your gadget to work out how much fabric you will need. There are three pieces to this project—back, front, and flap. The back needs to be the same size as your gadget plus ⅜ in. (1 cm) all around; the front piece is the same width and two-thirds of the height of the back piece; and the flap is the same width as the back and 4 in. (10 cm) deep. To make the cover more sturdy and provide extra padding, cut two of each piece. Round off the corners of each piece.

2 Trace the templates on page 123 onto copy or parchment paper and cut out. Use to cut out two hearts from red felt, two Dala horses from pink felt, and four little green leaves. Place them on the front panel. When you're happy with the positions, apply a tiny dot of fabric glue to the back of each one and gently press them in place. Using matching sewing thread, stitch the decorations in place.

3 I used a bright red bias binding to match the red hearts. It goes so well with light blue background and makes the whole design "pop." Pin the decorated front panel right side up on the plain front panel. Turn the panel over and pin the bias binding along the top edge, allowing an inch or so (a few centimetres) to stick out at each end. Machine stitch along the top crease line in the binding.

4 Trim the blue felt a little if necessary, and fold the bias binding over to the front. Sew along the edge of binding from the front. Attach bias binding to the bottom edge of the flap, too; don't forget to pin the two layers of the flap together before you start sewing.

5 Cut off any excess binding sticking out on the sides, leaving just ½ in. (1 cm) or so extending. Fold it over to the back of each piece and attach with a few hand stitches.

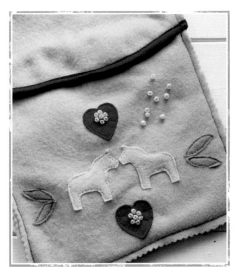

6 Now we come to the exciting part— the assembly! Place the two back pieces in front of you, add the decorated front panel, and then the flap. Align all pieces carefully; trim here and there if you need to, but mind you don't get carried away and cut off too much! Pin the pieces together with long dressmaker's pins. Slowly sew all around the cover, using red thread.

7 Snip around the blue felt with pinking shears to give the cover a pretty edge, taking great care not to snip through the binding. Using a sharp needle and matching embroidery floss (thread), add a small beaded "flower" to each of the hearts, made up of a light blue center surrounded by pink beads.

8 Add five beads to the closing flap— light blue in the center, then a pink one on each side, and finally a blue bead on each side of the pink. There we go— a very sweet Nordic cover for your favorite gadget!

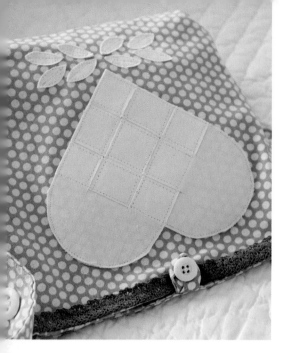

Over-the-shoulder BAG

To create something with your own hands to use in your everyday life is something very special indeed—you have the freedom to make it suit your individual color palette and style. I made a bag that fits me perfectly: cool Nordic colors with a large and classy Scandinavian statement in the shape of the braided heart, my favorite symbol. You can make this in under an hour and then go on a shopping trip to show it off to all your friends!

YOU WILL NEED

- Templates on page 123
- 32 x 27½ in. (80 x 70 cm) light blue and white polka-dot cotton fabric for the outer bag
- 85 x 3 in. (210 x 8 cm) light blue and white polka-dot cotton fabric for the straps
- 32 x 27½ in. (80 x 70 cm) light blue-and-white striped lining fabric
- 10-in. (25-cm) square white cotton fabric

- 10-in. (25-cm) square lightweight iron-on interfacing
- 12 in. (30 cm) gray/blue cotton lace, ¾ in. (20 mm) wide
- One white plastic button, ⁵⁄₁₆ in. (18 mm) in diameter
- Two white plastic buttons, ¾ in. (22 mm) in diameter
- White sewing thread
- Wooden spoon
- Basic kit (see page 120)

1 Copy the bag template on page 123 and use to cut out two bag panels from the polka-dot fabric.

2 Following the manufacturer's instructions, apply lightweight iron-on interfacing to the back of the white cotton fabric and cut out two half-hearts and eight little leaves. Braid (plait) the "fingers" over and under each other, following the instructions for the Braided Half Apron on page 42. Position the heart on the front of the bag, about 2 in. (5 cm) from the top and centered on the width, with the leaves in pairs underneath. Using white thread, machine stitch the heart to the front of the bag. Sew along both sides of each "finger," too, to keep them from moving around. Sew around each leaf and then down the middle to create the central "vein."

3 Choose a matching blue–gray cotton lace and iron it if necessary. Stitch it to the very top of the front panel, leaving 1 in. (2–3 cm) or so sticking out at each side.

4 Pin the front and back panels right sides together. Machine stitch along the side and bottom edges. Gather the "cut-out" corners together and lay them flat on top of each other pulling out into a straight line. Sew straight across on both sides of the bag.

5 Turn the bag right side out and carefully push out all corners and seams. Iron the bag a little, to make sure all parts are straight.

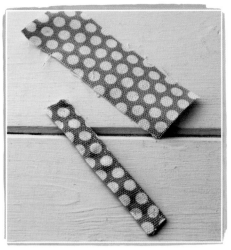

6 Now make the button strip. From the leftover fabric, cut a strip of polka-dot fabric measuring 3 x 1½ in. (8 x 4 cm). Fold over ⅜ in. (1 cm) to the wrong side along each long edge, then fold the strip in half and press again. Machine stitch along the long unfolded side.

7 Cut out two panels of lining fabric, the same size as the outer bag panels. Pin them right sides together and machine stitch the side seams only. Trim all loose thread ends. Place the outer bag inside the lining tube, with right sides together, and pin together along the top edge.

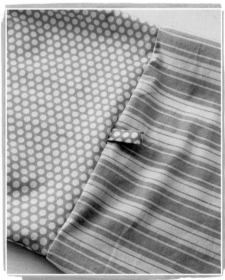

8 Fold the button strip in half lengthwise. Place it in the center of the back panel, between the two layers, with the loop pointing downward. Sew all around the opening, sewing over the button strip a few extra times to make sure it is fixed securely.

9 Pull the lining up over the bag, so that both lining and outer bag are right side out, and make sure the button strip is in the right position.

10 Close up the corners at the bottom of the lining, as you did on the outer bag in step 4.

11 Now make the strap. The material I had chosen was not long enough to make my strap in one go, so I cut six lengths each 14 in. (35 cm) long—three for each side of the strap. Round off the corners on one end of four of the lengths: in total you will need four rounded end strips and two straight middle strips. Taking a ⅜-in. (1-cm) seam allowance, stitch each middle strip to the straight ends of the two of the rounded strips. Press the seams open.

12 Pin the straps right sides together, aligning the edges carefully. Using pins, mark a 2½-in. (6-cm) gap along one long side: this is where you will start and stop sewing.

13 Sew all around the strap, then turn it right side out, using the handle of a wooden spoon to help you. Press the strap flat, then sew all around it twice, spacing the stitching lines about ¼ in. (6 mm) apart, to make it extra sturdy.

14 Buttons—I love them! You can take your pick and either go for a more restrained look with white buttons or go to town and add some blue splash! Here, I opted for white. Add one small white button to the center front of the bag, stitching it over the lace with white thread.

15 Also add one larger button to each side of the bag. Hold the end of the strap to the side of the bag and sew the button to the bag, stitching through the strap, bag, and lining. And there you are— a lovely new over-the-shoulder bag in less than an hour.

Child's SAMI-INSPIRED SLIPPERS

Growing up in the very south of Sweden, the Sami people of northern Scandinavia were a very exciting and exotic mystery to me—they dressed in fabulously colorful and embroidered clothing, lived outside in tents, and herded reindeers! Here I have created a pair of slippers that, to me, displays something of their style.

YOU WILL NEED

- Templates on page 123
- 14 x 9 in. (35 x 23 cm) dark gray felt
- 16 x 9 in. (40 x 23 cm) each of ruby red and mustard felt
- 8 x 5 in. (20 x 13 cm) 3-oz (125-g) batting (wadding)
- 1 yd (1 m) each of red and green jute string
- 1⅜ yd (1.2 m) of gray jute string
- 3 in. (8 cm) Sami ribbon, ⅜ in. (10 mm) wide
- Stick-on non-stick soles
- Green, yellow, and red embroidery floss (thread)
- Gray, red, and yellow sewing thread
- Basic kit (see page 120)

1 Trace the templates on page 123 onto copy or parchment paper and cut out (they fit a child aged 5 or 6, so you may need to enlarge or reduce them—see page 120). To make the slippers more sturdy, you will need two layers of felt for each part—so cut out four soles (two left and two right) from dark gray felt. Cut out a left and a right sole from batting (wadding), cutting it just a little bit smaller than the sole pieces.

2 Load your sewing machine with gray thread, place the two right sole pieces on top of each other with the batting (wadding) sandwiched in between, and carefully sew all around to make a soft, padded sole, making sure you catch the batting in with your stitching. Repeat with the left sole and batting pieces.

TOP TIP

Fold the felt in half and pin the layers together before you cut, so that you cut the soles out as identical pairs; no matter how careful you are, it's very difficult to cut out four individual pieces that align perfectly with each other.

3 As with the soles, you will need two layers for sturdiness—two for each side panel of each slipper. Pin the red and mustard-colored felts together, then lay the slipper template on top and cut out two double-layer panels. Flip the template over so that the shape is reversed, then cut out another two double-layer panels for the second side of the slippers.

4 Now make the tassels. Jute string is such a lovely, natural material—I use it for absolutely everything! Cut six 4-in. (10-cm) lengths each of red and gray jute string and one long length of red measuring 12 in. (30 cm). Place the short lengths together in a bundle, then wrap the longer piece around the center of the bundle and tie it in a knot.

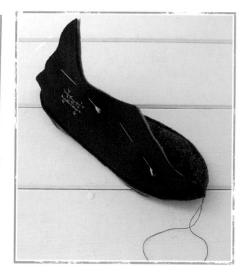

5 Push all the short strings downward and trim if they are uneven. Cut a 1½-in. (4-cm) piece of the ribbon. Wrap the ribbon tightly around the jute strings and fasten the end with a few blanket stitches in matching green embroidery floss (thread). Repeat steps 4 and 5 to make a green tassel.

6 The Sami are amazing at embroidering their garments in elaborate patterns; I am only a girl from southern Sweden, so I didn't dare to make it too complicated! I made up a very simple design of straight stitches in red and mustard, with green cross stitches at regular intervals, but you can create your own pattern if you prefer. Only sew on the red outer part of the front, so that you can conceal the stitches later with the mustard one. Decorate the outer side of each slipper only—so one slipper will be embroidered on the right-hand side, like here, and the other on the left.

7 Load your sewing machine with red thread. Pin the red and mustard felt pieces for the outside edge of one slipper together, then place them on a sole piece and stitch together, working from the tip of the toe to the heel.

8 Attach the undecorated set of red and mustard felt pieces to the inside edge of the slipper and sew along each top edge in turn, from the heel to the start of the foot opening.

TOP TIPS

Take your time and adjust the layers of felt, frequently so that they lie precisely on top of each other. You may find it easier to pin the upper pieces to the sole and remove the pins as you stitch.

I've found that jute string irons really well, so you can do that if you want to have a straighter tassel. Be very careful of your fingers, though!

9 Pull the four layers together at the heel. Trim them if they are uneven, then sew straight down from the top edge to the bottom.

10 Using a very sharp needle and red embroidery floss, blanket stitch (see page 121) the outside and inside edges together from the toe up to the top of the foot opening.

11 Place the tassel on the decorated side of the slipper and attach it with a few stitches on the machine, using yellow thread. Snip of the excess string with your scissors.

12 Fold the very back tip over by about ½ in. (1 cm) and sew it in place with a few stitches, just nipping the ruby red felt. Following the manufacturer's instructions, stick a non-slip sole onto the base of the slipper. Repeat steps 6–12 to make the second slipper.

Felt MEMORY GAME

Get away from the "electronics" for a while and play my version of the classic game, "Memory." Made out of soft felt, the play pieces are decorated with a loving heart theme on crisp, white cotton, which shows off the images perfectly. Make as many pairs as you like—you can even get the kids involved in the decorating and let them create their own personalized designs!

YOU WILL NEED

For 12 pairs of squares

- Approx. 1 sq. yd (90 sq. cm) each of light beige and dark gray felt
- Approx. 1 sq. yd (90 sq cm) of white cotton fabric
- Approx 1 sq. yd (90 sq cm) of iron-on interfacing
- Rubber stamps—a range of large and small designs
- Deep red, turquoise, olive green, and mustard ink pads
- White sewing thread
- Basic kit (see page 120)

Basic kit (see page 120)

TIP

Felt is quite hard to draw on, so I use large pins to mark the measurements instead. Try and keep the patches in the pairs that you cut them in so to speak, since they are identical.

1 For each play piece, you will need two layers of felt—so for every pair, you need to cut four patches, each one 2¾ in. (7 cm) square. Lay the felt double and cut out the squares with pinking shears to give them a pretty edge.

2 Press the white cotton fabric, then apply iron-on interfacing to the back of it, shiny side down. Mark out a 2½ in. (6.5-cm) square for each play piece—so you need two per pair. Leave them to one side for now.

3 Draw a 2-in. (5-cm) square on a white sheet of paper and cut it out; this will be your guide for cutting the windows in the play patches. Place the square in the center of one of the felt pieces and, using a soft pencil or tailor's chalk, draw around it—just make sure you don't pull the felt out of shape. Mark an "X" in the middle of the square, and cut it out. Take particular care in the corners, making them crisp.

4 Find some pretty heart stamps, plus some smaller decorative stamps and go to town! Stamp out pairs of designs on the white cotton squares, using whatever motifs and colors you like. Remember that the white patch is larger than the window, so keep the decorations in the center.

5 Place each decorated cotton patch on a whole felt square. Apply a little bit of glue to the back of the frame, then place the frame on top of the cotton patch. Press down firmly.

6 With white thread, stitch all around the square once, then zig-zag stitch the image in place, with your stitches overlapping the inner edge of the frame and the white cotton. Finally, add another line of straight stitches just outside the first, trim all loose thread ends, and call the kids to come and play!

Child's FELT BAG

Having your own shopping bag or purse when you are a child is just the best thing—and it's extra special if your mum or dad have made it for you! In Scandinavia, red and white houses are literally everywhere and I recently made this little bag for my own daughter as a reminder of our heritage when we go shopping together.

YOU WILL NEED

- Templates on page 124
- Three 8 x 5¾-in. (20.5 x 14.5-cm) sheets of light blue felt
- Scraps of red, white, and green felt
- White or natural ric-rac braid, 1½ –2 in. (4–5 cm) long
- Snap fastener
- Blue, black, and red gingham ribbons ⅜ in. (1 cm) wide for the strap
- Two matt silver eyelets
- White and green sewing threads
- Light blue embroidery floss (thread)
- Hole punch
- Eyelet setting tool
- Basic kit (see page 120)

1 Trace the templates on page 124 onto copy or parchment paper and cut them out. Use to cut out all the pieces from the relevant color of felt and lay them out on one of the light blue felt sheets to make sure you're happy with the design. Use pinking shears to cut the underside of the roof.

2 Using white sewing thread, stitch on the house, windows, door, and the two flower parts. For the flower stem and two leaves, use green sewing thread.

3 Now take the other two felt rectangles. Lay one out lengthwise in front of you, and overlap the other one on top, covering the top 3¾ in. (9.5 cm). Using white thread, machine stitch along the two lines where the rectangles overlap.

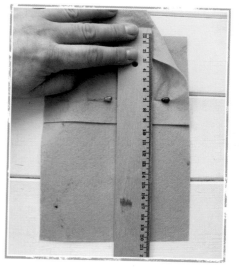

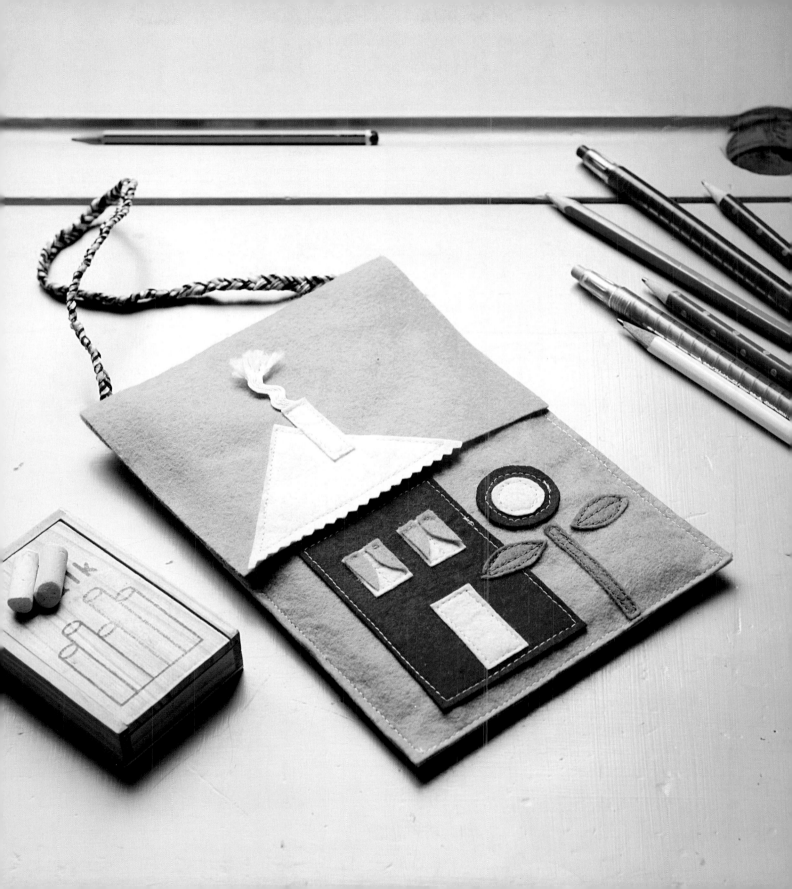

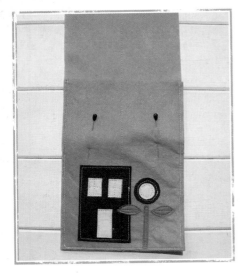

4 Place the front piece right side up on top of the "double" piece you've just created, lining them up carefully along the side and bottom edges, and pin in place. Machine stitch around the side and bottom edges of the front piece, using white sewing thread.

5 Fold the top part of the "double" piece over to the front; this will become the flap of the bag. Place the roof at the very edge of the flap, overlapping it just a little, and pin it in place.

6 Sew around the entire roof with white sewing thread and trim all loose ends. Place the chimney on the right side of the roof and with a short length of ric-rac braid underneath it, sticking out by about 1¼ in. (3 cm), and sew around the chimney. Fluff out the end of the ric-rac apart a little so that it looks like smoke.

7 Attach the snap fastener, sewing one half on the inside of the flap and the other just above the little house. Before you sew on anything, make sure the two will meet when the lid is closed! Fold over the flap, making sure all sides meet as they should when you close the snap fastener.

8 Use a hole punch to make one hole on each side of the back of the back, making sure you only pierce through the two back layers. Set a matt silver eyelet in each of the holes.

9 Depending on how long you want the strap to be, cut three lengths of gingham ribbon—one blue, one red, and one black. Tie the top ends together and braid (plait) them together. When you're about 2 in. (5 cm) from the end, push the ribbons through the left-hand eyelet, from the front to the back. Now tie the ends together and you pull the knot really tight. Untie the knot on the other end of the braid, feed it through the right-hand eyelet, and knot the end again.

10 Finally, hand stitch pretty blue curtains to the windows, using blue embroidery floss (thread).

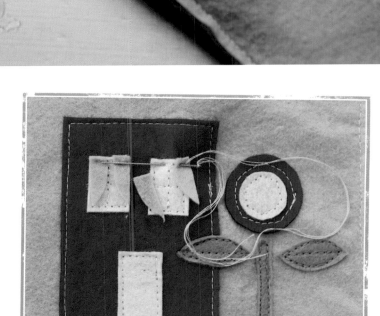

Norwegian FOREST KITTENS

The Norwegian Forest cat is a beautiful and majestic creature. It is one of the larger types of cat, with a long, soft coat, and is famous for the cute little tufts of hair at the very tips of its ears, protecting them from the harsh Nordic winter. No one can resist a bunch of little kittens and these Norwegian-inspired felines are so sweet and easy to make, you are sure to make a whole litter!

YOU WILL NEED

- Template on page 124
- Approx. 7 x 5½ in. (18 x 14 cm) felt in your chosen color for the kitten's body
- Scraps of blue, green, yellow, and white felt for the eyes and patches
- Embroidery flosses (threads) to match the felt colors
- Polyester toy filling
- Wooden spoon
- Basic kit (see page 120)

1 Trace the template on page 124 onto copy or parchment paper and cut it out. Fold your chosen color of felt in half, pin the template to it, and cut out your first little kitten.

2 Cut out two pairs of ovals for your kitten's eyes—one blue or green pair and one yellow.

3 Place them on the kitten, with the blue or green eyes horizontal and the yellow eyes vertical, creating an "X." Sew in place with black embroidery floss (thread).

4 Cut out the kitten's patches and strips of color freehand—they look more natural that way. Lay them out in the design you prefer. Attach the pieces by hand, using matching embroidery floss (thread) and regular straight stitches.

5 Change to a silver-gray floss and work a triangle of stitches to give the little fellow a nose, followed by three or four straight stitches on either side of the nose for the whiskers. Sew two straight stitches downward and lastly one diagonal stitch on each side of the lower stitch to complete the mouth.

6 Lay the front and back kitten pieces on top of each other, aligning them carefully, and pin them together. Pick a contrasting color of embroidery floss (thread) and join the two pieces together by working blanket stitch (see page 121) from the bottom of one side all the way around to the bottom of the other side, leaving the base open—but don't snip off the thread. Stuff the kitten with toy filling, pushing it in with the handle of a wooden spoon, then blanket stitch the gap closed.

7 Thread your needle with one strand each of two different colors of floss (thread). Sew the tufts at the very top of the ears, just pushing the needle through and leaving a loop instead of finishing the stitch. Secure the threads each time with a tiny stitch.

8 Snip the loops open and trim the lengths if necessary. Then make a litter of little friends for your Norwegian Forest kitten to play with!

Child's VINTAGE APRON

This sweet little apron was inspired by my favorite painting by Swedish artist Carl Larsson, "A Late Riser's Miserable Breakfast", in which the little girl sits grumpily at the breakfast table wearing an apron very similar to the one I have created. She is adorable! For my own daughter, I have made plain ones, striped ones, and checkered ones—Scandinavian vintage-style aprons to fit over any dress.

YOU WILL NEED

- Templates on page 124
- ¾ yd (50 cm) cotton fabric 60 in. (150 cm) wide in your chosen color and/or pattern for the apron
- ¾ yd (50 cm) cotton fabric 60 in. (150 cm) wide white cotton fabric for the lining
- Approx. 6 in. (15 cm) square of white linen (or your chosen color and/or pattern) for the heart appliqué
- Approx. 6 in. (15 cm) square of iron-on lightweight interfacing
- Two wooden flower-shaped buttons, ⅜ in. (10 mm) in diameter
- White sewing thread
- Pink embroidery floss (thread)
- Basic kit (see page 120)

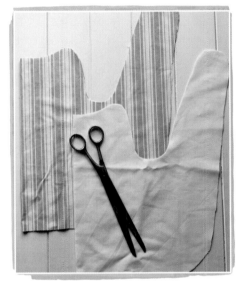

1 Copy the templates on page 124 and cut out. Fold your apron fabric in half and press to mark a crease in the middle—this is so that you end up with two identical sides. With the fabric still folded, place the straight edge of the apron template on the crease and pin it in place. Cut out the apron, cutting through both layers. Repeat with the white cotton material—but this time, cut a tiny bit outside the template, so that it's just a little bit bigger than the apron part.

2 Fold a 16 x 12-in. (40 x 30-cm) piece of the apron fabric in half and cut out a little pocket, using the pocket template. Cut around the round part with pinking shears.

3 Following the manufacturer's instructions, apply iron-on interfacing to the back of the linen fabric for the heart. Using the half-heart template, cut out the two parts of the heart. Braid (plait) the heart in the same way as for the Braided Half Apron on page 42, then trim off any edges that stick out a little longer than the others. Place the braided heart in the center of the pocket and machine stitch around it with white sewing thread.

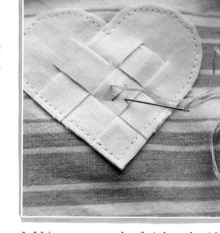

4 Using two strands of pink embroidery floss (thread), work one cross stitch onto the second square up from the base of the heart.

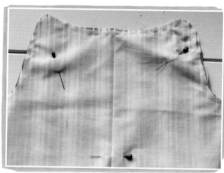

6 Place the apron right side up, then place the white cotton lining on top, aligning all the edges. Pin the two layers together. It doesn't matter if the lining is a little larger than the apron material, but it should not be any smaller, or it will sew unevenly. Machine stitch almost all around the apron, leaving a gap of 2 in. (5 cm) at the bottom. Turn the apron right side out through the gap and slipstitch (see pages 121) the gap closed. Press the apron carefully, making sure that all the edges line up and no lining shows from the back.

5 Now pin the pocket to the center front of the apron and machine stitch it in place; sew two parallel lines of stitching about ¼ in. (6 mm) apart to attach it really securely.

7 Sew one wooden flower-shaped button to the top of each front "strap." On each back "strap," sew a small buttonhole and open it carefully with a seam ripper.

Patchwork TIC-TAC-TOE

Whether it's on the beach or in the woods, summer in Scandinavia equals picnics. Load the baskets with homemade delicacies such as meatball sandwiches, potato salads, seafood quiches, and, of course, something sweet! When everyone has eaten their fill, it's time to relax and to play games. Here I have made a portable tic-tac-toe game to celebrate the Nordic summer—mosquitoes and all!

YOU WILL NEED

- 31 assorted 4-in. (10-cm) squares of patterned fabric (18 for the tic-tac-toe board, 10 for the game pieces, and 3 for the bag decoration)
- 10 x 12 in. (25 x 30 cm) white cotton fabric for the bag
- 10 x 12 in. (25 x 30 cm) lightweight iron-on interfacing for the bag
- 12 x 8 in. (30 x 20 cm) fusible bonding web for the game pieces

- 20 in. (50 cm) each of red, blue, green, and yellow gingham ribbon for the tic-tac-toe board
- 27½ in. (70 cm) each of yellow and blue gingham ribbon for the bag
- Six yellow and green flower-shaped grommets (eyelets)
- Grommet (eyelet) tool
- Matching sewing thread
- Basic kit (see page 120)

1 You will need nine squares per side to make the tic-tac-toe board, so cut out 18 different squares measuring 4 in. (10 cm) each. Decide on your design first by laying out the squares in two groups of 3 x 3. I always find it useful to take a snapshot on my camera or mobile phone that I can refer to later.

2 Take the squares for your top row of patches. With right sides together, taking a ⅜-in. (1-cm) seam allowance, stitch the squares together. Press the seams to one side. Repeat to make the remaining rows, keeping a careful note of which rows are for the back of the board and which are for the front.

3 Press the rows of patches flat. With right sides together, carefully aligning the seams, pin the top row of the board front to the center row and machine stitch, taking a ⅜ in. (1-cm) seam allowance. Attach the bottom row to the center row in the same way. Press the seams to one side. Now do the same with the remaining rows to create the back of the board.

4 With right sides together, pin the back and front of the board together and machine stitch, taking a ⅜-in. (1-cm) seam allowance and leaving a 4-in. (10-cm) gap in one side. Turn the board right side out through the gap, gently push out the corners, and press it flat. Turn in the seam allowance along the gap and stitch all around the outer edges of the board with white thread to close it all up.

TOP TIP

If the ribbon on the first side "kinks" when you're stitching the second set of ribbons to the back, just snip off the stitches that are holding your ribbon folded and sew a few stitches over it to fasten it in place again.

5 Gingham thread is so cheery and gives everything such a happy tone. Cut two 10-in. (25-cm) lengths of each color and snip the ends into a "V-shape" with a sharp scissors. Pin two ribbons of the same color over the vertical seams on the front of the board. Using white thread, machine stitch along the center of each ribbon. Repeat on the horizontal seams, using a different color of ribbon. Turn the game over and attach the other two colors of ribbon in the same way.

6 Now make the bag to hold your game. From three different patterned fabrics, cut freehand two "X" and one "O". Cut two pieces of white cotton fabric measuring 8 x 5 in. (20 x 13 cm) for the bag. Following the manufacturer's instructions, apply lightweight iron-on interfacing to the back of each one. Using white thread, machine stitch the letters to the bag front.

7 Along the top edge of each bag piece, fold over ⅜ in. (1 cm) to the wrong side and press. Machine stitch straight across. Pin the front and back of the bag right sides together and machine stitch, taking a ⅜-in. (1-cm) seam allowance. Trim all loose thread ends and turn the bag right side out. Gently push out the corners and press the bag flat. Select six small grommets (eyelets) and set them at the top of the bag—three on the front and three on the back—spacing them evenly.

8 Cut a 27½-in. (70-cm) length each of yellow and blue gingham ribbon. Gather the two ends and carefully feed them through the grommets (eyelets) from the right side of the back, weaving them in and out and finishing on the right side of the front. Adjust so that the same amount of ribbon protrudes at each end, then snip the ends in a "V-shape."

9 To make each game piece, cut two 4-in. (10-cm) squares of the same fabric. Following the manufacturer's instructions, apply fusible bonding web to the back of one square, then peel off the backing paper and fuse that square to the back of the other square, using a hot iron. Working freehand, cut one "X" and one "O" out of each square. Make another four fabric patches in the same way, so that you have five Xs and five Os to play with.

Matchbox PETS

Having grown up in the middle of a dense Swedish forest, I encountered and studied all kinds of fantastic animals in the wild. Here I have recreated just a few of the species you might associate with Scandinavia along with a woodland "home from home" in a matchbox.

YOU WILL NEED

- Templates on page 124
- 6-in. (15-cm) square each of gray, brown, green, red, white, and natural felt
- Matching embroidery flosses (threads), plus black, white, and light gray
- Black, brown, and white round beads, 3 mm in diameter
- Polyester toy filling
- Basic kit (see page 120)

Trace the templates on page 124 onto copy or parchment paper and cut out. Fold the appropriate color of felt for the animals' bodies in half, pin the body templates to it, and cut out. Cut out all the facial features for each animal from the appropriate color of felt.

TO MAKE THE WILD BOAR

1 Place the boar's snout on one head piece and fix it in place by stitching on two round black beads for the nostrils, using black embroidery floss (thread). Add two more black beads for the eyes in the same way.

2 Sew two small tusks just above the snout with light gray embroidery floss (thread); isn't he sweet?

3 Place the decorated head on top of the back. Pin the two layers together, then blanket stitch around it with medium-gray floss (thread), leaving a small gap. Fill the head with toy filling, then stitch the gap closed. Do the same with the body.

4 Attach the head to the body with a few small hand stitches and your first little pet is ready!

TO MAKE THE BADGER

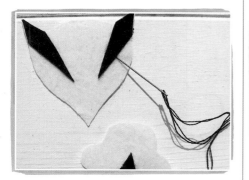

1 Place the distinctive black stripes on the badger's face and chest. Stitch the stripes in place by hand, using black embroidery floss (thread) and simple straight stitches. Stitch on three round black beads for the eyes and nose.

2 Place the decorated piece on top of the back. Pin the two layers together, then blanket stitch around with white floss (thread), leaving a small gap. Fill the head with toy filling, then stitch the gap closed. Do the same with the body. Attach the head to the body with a few small hand stitches.

TO MAKE THE SQUIRREL

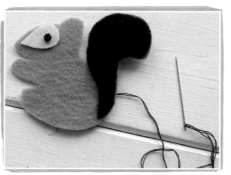

1 Place the squirrel's white facial stripe on one head piece and fix it in place by stitching on a round black bead for the eye, using black embroidery floss (thread). Now change to dark brown embroidery floss and stitch the fluffy brown tail onto the body, using simple straight stitches.

2 Place the decorated piece on top of the back. Pin the two layers together, then blanket stitch around with brown floss (thread), leaving a small gap. Fill with toy filling, then stitch the gap closed.

TO MAKE THE LYNX

1 Place the white mouth piece in the center of the face and attach it by sewing a nose and mouth with brown embroidery floss (thread). Also give him two eyes, attaching brown beads with the same color of floss.

2 Place the decorated piece on top of the back. Pin the two layers together, sandwiching a small wedge of felt on each side of the face for the tufted ears, then blanket stitch around with brown floss (thread), leaving a small gap. Fill with toy filling, then stitch the gap closed. Carefully snip a few slits in each of the ears to make them look extra fluffy.

TO MAKE THE TOADSTOOL

1 Cut out two red toadstool caps and two white stalks. Add a few white beads to one cap, then place the two caps together and blanket stitch around the curved top edge with red embroidery floss (thread), leaving the bottom edge open.

2 Blanket stitch the two layers of the white stalk together, adding a little toy filling before you stitch it shut. Place the top of the stalk in the open toadstool cap and stitch the two together.

TO MAKE THE TREE

1 Cut out all the tree pieces and attach one trunk to each of the green tree-top pieces, using short straight stitches and a contrasting color of thread. Place the two trees wrong sides together. Using green embroidery floss (thread) blanket stitch the two layers together, leaving the trunk and bottom edge of the green section open.

2 Fill the tree with toy filling, then close up the green part of the tree, leaving the trunks hanging loose for now.

3 Blanket stitch the two trunks together, using brown floss (thread).

FOR YOUR PETS' FOREST HOME

Matchboxes in themselves are sadly not very decorative, so cut pretty paper to size and glue it carefully around the matchbox cover. You can also paint the inner base of the matchbox in forest greens if you want, and let it dry. Add dried twigs, moss, leaves, and flowers to create a really magical environment for your little pets!

Love birds MOBILE

Many of us have inherited lovely tablecloths or other home furnishings from family or friends, and even though they are beautiful and of great sentimental value, there are only so many you can use in a day! So instead of them lying hidden in a dark closet, make something new out of them to decorate your home. I've loved this particular fabric for years—but now it's time to turn it into something new—a cute decorative mobile hat will brighten up any child's room.

YOU WILL NEED

- Templates on page 124
- 5 x 7 in. (12 x 18 cm) retro-style floral fabric for the birds
- 3 x 4 in. (7 x 10 cm) each of two retro-style spotted fabrics for the heart
- 8-in. (20-cm) square of natural cotton fabric
- 8-in. (20-cm) square of lightweight iron-on interfacing
- 32 in. (80 cm) blue-and-yellow ribbon, ⅝ in. (15 mm) wide
- 42 in. (105 cm) blue-and-white gingham ribbon, ⅜ in. (10 mm) wide
- 1¾ yd (1.6 m) white fluffy yarn
- Polyester toy filling
- Sewing threads to match your fabrics
- White coated metal hoop 7 in. (18 cm) in diameter
- Superglue
- Basic kit (see page 120)

1 Trace the templates on page 124 onto copy or parchment paper and cut them out. Following the manufacturer's instructions, apply iron-on interfacing to the back of all the patterned fabrics. Cut out two birds from floral fabric (make sure you flip the template so that you get them facing each other) and one half-heart shape from each spotted fabric; from natural cotton, cut two wings (again flipping the template). Using pinking shears, cut out two slightly larger birds and a complete heart from natural cotton.

2 Load your sewing machine with dark blue thread and attach the two little wings by sewing around them a couple of times. Pin each bird to a natural cotton backing piece.

 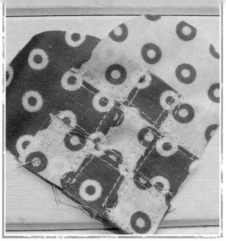 

3 Thread your machine with white thread and sew around the birds, leaving a small gap at the bottom. Fill the birds with toy filling. Place them back on your sewing machine, close up the gap, and trim off all thread ends.

4 Braid (plait) the heart in the same way as for the Braided Half Apron on page 42, then trim off any edges that stick out a little longer than the others. Also carefully sew along both sides of each "finger," to keep them from moving around. Trim all loose thread ends and pin the heart to its natural cotton backing piece.

5 Assemble the heart the same way as you did the birds; add stuffing, then sew the heart shut. Now you have two sweet little birds and a typically Scandinavian braided heart.

6 To make the hanging loop, cut a 16-in. (40-cm) length of ribbon. Fold it over the metal hoop and hold the raw ends of the ribbon together, folding in ½ in. (1 cm or so) of each raw end for a neater finish. Carefully box stitch (see page 121) over the raw ends of the ribbon, using dark blue thread.

7 Pull the ribbon taut, then stitch across it 5 in. (12.5 cm) from the bottom of the loop.

8 Cut two more lengths of ribbon, each 8 in. (20 cm) long. Fold them over the metal hoop and box stitch the raw ends, as before.

9 Thread your sewing needle with dark blue thread and hand stitch the little birds securely to their hangers. Then do the same with the heart.

10 Hold the hanger straight up in front of you and mark where the ribbons should be glued for them to hang outward at a slight angle. Add a tiny bit of Superglue to the inside of each ribbon loop and press them down onto the metal ring.

11 To dress the metal hoop, wind white fluffy yarn around it, starting by tying it "inside" the hanging tab at the top. Wind the yarn around the hoop quite tightly, so it does not slide until you come back to the start and tie it inside the tab again. Make sure the yarn is evenly spread out and does not move around.

12 Cut seven 6-in. (15-cm) lengths of blue-and-white gingham ribbon. Snip the ends in a "V", fold them in half, and loop them around the metal hoop, and then thread the ends through the loop—one between the two birds and three on each side of the hoop. Pull tight and then we're finished!

Felt cinnamon BUNS

In Scandinavia, one of our "staple foods" is our famous cinnamon bun! Since the early 1920s, this sweet and sticky delicacy has made countless mouths salivate with its intense fragrances of hot cinnamon, butter, and sugar. We love it so much, it even has its own day—4 October. As children we all loved playing tea parties and it was so much fun to make cups of tea for the whole family. If you were lucky enough to have real buns to play with, your day was made! Here I have created a whole bunch of yummy Scandinavian cinnamon buns, complete with sweet pearl sugar—I dare you not to pick one up and smell it! Cinnamon buns come in a wonderful array of brown and white tones, so find a few different shades for this project.

YOU WILL NEED

- Felt in varying shades of brown and beige—hazelnut, sand, chocolate, and natural white—approx. 12 x 3 in. (30 x 7.5 cm) each of three different shades per bun
- Various sizes of round white beads
- White sewing thread
- Basic kit (see page 120)

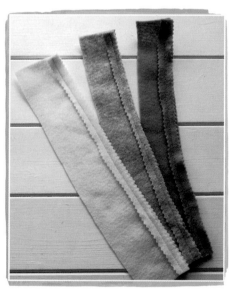

1 To make one bun, you need three long strips in three different tones. From each color of felt, cut one strip measuring 2 x 12 in. (5 x 30 cm), then cut one long edge of the strip with pinking shears. To create a little bit of upper "bulk," also cut a ⅜ x 12-in. (1 x 30-cm) strip from each color. Cut both long edges of this strip with the pinking shears.

2 Place each narrow strip on the wider strip of the same color along the pinked long edge and sew them together.

3 Now place the finished strips on top of each other and align them well. Sew all along the long unpinked edge to join all three strips together.

4 Before you roll the bun together, make sure you have a needle and thread ready; if you let go, the bun will unravel itself fairly rapidly! Roll the bun up, then blanket stitch (see page 121) the end of the bun to the side. You will probably need to snip off a few bits at the end to get a neat edge before you sew the bun together.

5 Once the bun is assembled, look at the underside and cut away any protruding bits to that the bun will stand straight.

6 Using a sharp needle and white sewing thread, add white beads in different sizes here and there, making sure that the white thread doesn't show on the bun itself. I defy you not to go and bake the real thing now! You can almost smell the fabulous fragrance of cardamom and cinnamon—irresistible!

Chapter 4 CELEBRATIONS

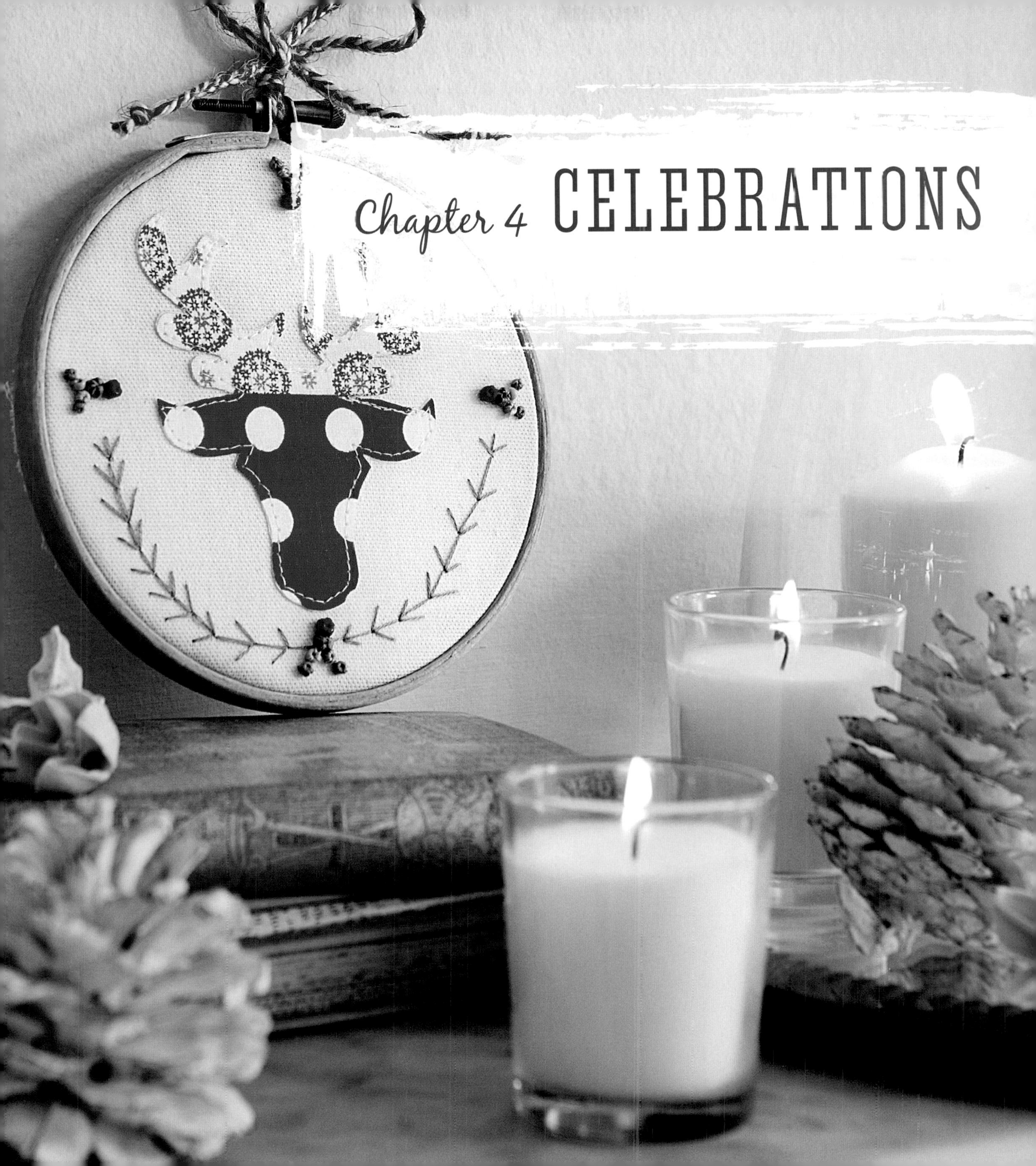

Nordic EASTER CHICKS

In Scandinavia, celebrating Easter without little chicks decorating everything in sight is simply unthinkable! Here's how to make two little yellow pals to brighten up your spring home!

YOU WILL NEED

- Nine 4-in. (10-cm) squares of two small-print floral cotton fabrics (five squares of fabric A and four of fabric B)
- Yellow crocheted cotton doily, 8 in. (20 cm) in diameter ★
- Scraps of red felt
- 12-in. (30-cm) square of lightweight iron-on interfacing
- Four black round beads, 3 mm in diameter
- 10 in. (25 cm) red gingham ribbon, ⅜ in. (10 mm) wide
- Yellow/orange, black, and red embroidery floss (thread)
- White and yellow sewing thread
- Spray adhesive
- Basic kit (see page 120)
- ★ Note: You can easily find crocheted doilies in all kinds of colors in flea markets, but if you cannot find one, you can dye a plain white one instead.

1 Lay out the squares in the following order: Row 1: A, B, A; row 2: B, A, B; row 3: A, B, A. With right sides together, taking a ⅜-in. (1-cm) seam allowance, machine stitch the squares in each row together, then press the seams to one side. Then stitch the rows together, carefully aligning the seams. Press the seams to one side.

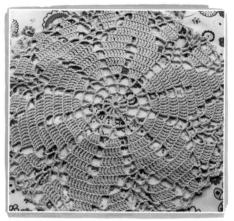

2 Lightly spray the front of the patchwork with adhesive and center the doily on it. Gently smooth it out and press it down. Load your sewing machine with matching yellow thread and sew around the doily in three or four concentric circles to attach it to the patchwork square.

3 From the front, sew two parallel lines across the center of the doily, spacing them ⅜ in. (1 cm) apart. Using sharp scissors, cut straight across the doily between the two lines so that you have two semicircles. Trim off the excess patchwork material, leaving just a tiny amount beyond the doily.

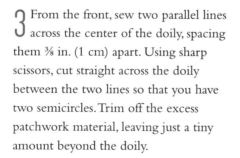

4 Following the manufacturer's instructions, apply lightweight iron-on interfacing to the back of the two semicircles, then trim off any excess as before.

5 For each chick, cut two small right-angle triangles of red felt. Thread your machine with red thread, then stitch them to the front of a semicircle as shown, stitching along only one edge.

6 Fold the triangles up so that the edges meet. Using red embroidery floss (thread), hand stitch the edges together. Using black embroidery floss, sew on two black beads for the eyes.

TOP TIP

Be sure to use a very sharp needle, since you need to get through cotton fabric, interfacing, and doily!

7 Cut about 5 in. (13 cm) of red gingham ribbon. Hold the two ends together between your fingers and carefully push in the middle of the "bubble" between the ribbon ends. Hold on tight, because it is easy to let go of them! Sew the bottom of the ribbon together on your sewing machine, taking care to stitch through all layers.

8 Fold the bottom of the ribbons in half widthwise and hand stitch it to the back of the patchwork just above the eyes, using yellow thread.

9 Fold the semicircle in half along the straight edge to form a cone, then hand stitch from the top down to the bottom and secure the thread well. Repeat steps 6–9 to finish the other chick.

Rustic
FELT HEART DECORATIONS

Hanging little hearts in your home, whatever the season, is almost a must for the Scandinavian household—we do love our heart decorations! They add a warmth to a home that puts any visitor at ease. Why not make an extra set for your guests as a lovely parting gift for them adorn their own home?

YOU WILL NEED

- Flat-backed wooden "discs," ⅜ in. (1 cm) in diameter
- Red and white acrylic paints
- Templates on page 125
- Dark blue, red, yellow, green, and white felt
- 8-in. (20-cm) lengths of red and yellow gingham ribbons, ⅜ in. (10 mm) wide
- Red and yellow sewing threads
- White embroidery floss (thread)
- Paintbrush
- Basic kit (see page 120)

> ### TIP
> *If you find the snowflakes too fiddly to draw and cut out, look for ready-made felt snowflakes on the Internet.*

1 Start by decorating the little wooden discs—they will need quite a while to dry, so get them done before you start sewing. Place a small drop of red acrylic paint in the middle of the disc, and then quickly add a smaller white drop, which merges with the red paint a little. Set aside for a few hours to dry.

2 Trace the templates on page 125 onto copy or parchment paper and cut out. Draw around the heart template twice on dark blue felt, then cut out the shapes. Cut out one snowflake motif from white felt.

3 Dab a little glue onto the back of a white felt snowflake and place it in the center of one of the blue hearts. Load your sewing machine with red thread and sew three straight separate lines across the snowflake to attach it to the felt, making sure that the lines cross in the middle.

4 Cut an 8-in. (20-cm) length of ribbon, fold it in half, and place it in the center of the second blue heart. Place the decorated heart right side up on top and pin it securely in place.

5 Machine stitch around the heart about ⅛ in. (3 mm) from the edge. I find it best to start sewing just on top of where the ribbon is placed and continue around from there; this way it won't have moved by the time you get back to your starting point.

6 When the painted wooden disc is fully dry, dab a little glue onto the back of it and place it in the center of the snowflake.

VARIATION

Assemble the red heart decorations in the same way, replacing the wooden disc and snowflake with a folkart-style flower, with a yellow center and green "petals", with four tiny circles of white felt interspersed between the "petals."

Winter teas with
HANDMADE GIFT TAGS

In the bitterly cold and dark days of winter, a good cup of tea is the best medicine for just about any ailment! Here I show you how to create a personal and thoughtful gift, which the recipient will treasure for a long time. Making your own gift labels is so much more fun than buying them ready made!

YOU WILL NEED

- Template on page 125 or tag-shaped craft punch
- Thick cream paper or thin cardstock
- Letter stamps
- Pretty border stamp
- Red and olive-green ink pads
- 4-in. (10-cm) square of cotton fabric per gift tag
- 4-in. (10-cm) square of iron-on interfacing per gift tag
- Red sewing thread
- Green and red raffia
- Hole punch
- Craft scissors
- Basic kit (see page 120)

1 Trace the template on page 125 onto paper and cut out. Using the template, cut out a tag from thick cream paper or thin cardstock; alternatively, punch out a tag using a craft punch of your choice. Punch a hole at the top using the hole punch. Find some pretty letters in a font that you like and stamp the name of the recipient on the tag. Add a sweet border stamp below the name, to give it that extra-special wintery Nordic touch.

2 Following the manufacturer's instructions, apply iron-on interfacing to the back of your chosen fabric; it needs that bit of extra support, otherwise the fabric will flap down on the outer sides of the tag later. Place your printed tag on a square of the strengthened material and machine stitch all around it; I used red thread to match the stamped lettering.

3 Trim all thread ends and cut around your label with a patterned craft scissors, following the shape of the tag. Place the hole punch in the hole you made earlier and now press through the fabric as well; take care and get the hole straight, since it would be a great shame to mess up at this late stage!

4 Depending on how wide your chosen glass jar is, cut a length of
raffia long enough to wrap five times around the neck of the jar. Fold
the raffia in half, push it though the hole in the tag, then feed the loose
ends of the raffia through the loop and pull taut. Now, wind your raffia
twice around the jar and finish off with a pretty bow. I filled my glass jar
with winterberry and chamomile and honey teas, which smell just
gorgeous when you open the jar!

Winter HOOP

A Scandinavian home at Christmas will not be lacking in reindeer decorations, that's for sure—reindeer hold a special place in our hearts! These beautiful animals roam the northern landscapes in herds of thousands and still provide many of the Sami people with vital income. And, of course, Santa would have a tough job delivering all those presents without their help! They also appear as key figures in many Norse myths: the stag Eikthrynir, for example, is credited with creating the world's rivers, which run down from the dew gathered on his antlers. Here I've made a lovely Christmas reindeer wall hanging, with bold fabrics, simple appliqué, and a bit of embroidery.

YOU WILL NEED

- Templates on page 125
- Embroidery hoop, 5½ in. (14 cm) in diameter
- Approx. 4 x 3 in. (10 x 8 cm) red-and-white polka-dot fabric for the reindeer head
- Approx. 4 x 3 in. (10 x 8 cm) wintery-patterned fabric on a white background for the reindeer horns
- 10-in. (25-cm) square of natural calico cotton fabric
- Four round red beads, 3 mm in diameter
- 20 round green glass beads
- 60 in. (150 cm) red-and-white baker's twine
- Green and red embroidery floss (thread)
- White sewing thread
- Basic kit (see page 120)

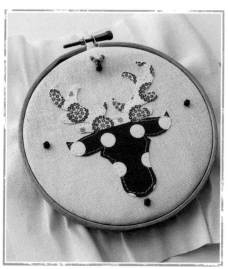

1 Trace the templates on page 125 onto copy or parchment paper and cut out. Use to cut out the head and horns from fabric. With right sides together, using white sewing thread, machine stitch the horns to the top of the head, then press the seam open. Stitch the reindeer to the calico, again using white thread, and then mount the fabric in the embroidery hoop, making sure that the image is centered.

2 At the four "points of the compass", sew on a red bead using red embroidery floss (thread). At each point, sew on five green beads; the first one directly above the red bead and the rest in sets of two, pointing diagonally outward from the red bead, using green floss (thread).

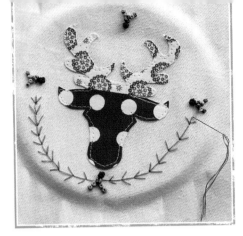

3 Take the material out of the hoop. Thread an embroidery needle with green floss. Starting from the bottom set of beads, sew a line of fern stitches (see page 121) in a curve up to the left set of beads. Do the same on the other side. The indentation left by the hoop provides you with a great guide to where to place the stitches!

4 Remount the fabric on the hoop, leaving the fastening screw at the very top, and pull the material taut. Turn the hoop over and check that there are no folds in the material. Using pinking shears, carefully cut away the excess fabric at the back of the hoop.

5 For some reason, nothing says "Christmas" to me quite like red and white baker's twine—it is so gorgeous and can (and should) be used to make everything wintery prettier! Cut three 20-in. (50-cm) lengths, and braid (plait) them together. Fold the braided twine in half and loop it around the fastening screw at the top of the hoop. Tie the twine in a pretty little bow and you're done!

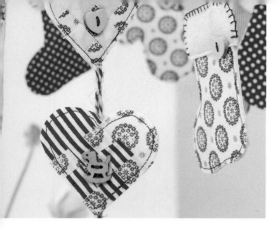

Christmas MOBILE

At the risk of sounding extremely biased, I have to say that a Scandinavian home dressed for Christmas is one of the most gorgeous images there is to see. Nordic houses are filled top to bottom with lit candles, lingonberry branches, and beautiful decorations—all in strong reds, whites, and greens. This mobile captures all of that for me and I'm sure you will love it, too.

YOU WILL NEED

- Templates on page 125
- Assortment of Christmassy Scandinavian-style cotton fabrics: 8 x 6 in. (20 x 15 cm) each of striped and polka-dot fabrics and 12 x 6 in. (30 x 15 cm) snowflake fabric
- 10 x 20 in. (25 x 50 cm) white felt
- 3 x 2 in. (8 x 5 cm) white cotton fabric
- 22 x 12 in. (55 x 30 cm) lightweight iron-on interfacing
- 4 yd (3.7 m) red-and-white baker's twine
- Seven mini wooden clothespins
- White coated metal hoop, 7 in. (18 cm) in diameter
- 2⅝ yd (2.4 m) red-and-white ribbon, ⅝ in. (15 mm) wide
- Three wooden rocking-horse buttons, 1 in. (25 mm) in diameter
- Three wooden heart-shaped buttons, ⅜ in. (10 mm) in diameter
- Three wooden Christmas-tree buttons, ¾ in. (20 mm) tall
- One clear plastic bead, ⅜ in. (10 mm) in diameter
- Red embroidery floss (thread)
- Red and white sewing threads
- Tapestry needle
- Basic kit (see page 120)

1 Trace the templates on page 125 onto copy or parchment paper and cut out. Use to cut out two mittens, two stockings, and two half-hearts from each of the striped, polka-dot, and snowflake fabrics. Cut another four half-hearts from the snowflake fabric and two half-heart from white cotton fabric. Following the manufacturer's instructions, apply lightweight iron-on interfacing to all the cut out pieces. Lay all the pieces on white felt and cut out identical pieces to use as backing in the next step.

2 Make sure you keep the pairs of fabric together; if you mix them up, they are likely not to fit together too well. Braid (plait) the hearts in the same way as for the Braided Half Apron on page 42, then trim off any edges that stick out a little longer than the others. Load your sewing machine with red thread and stitch around the edge of each decoration to attach it to the felt.

3 Fold the white felt in half. Using the templates, cut out three mitten cuffs and three stocking cuffs. Blanket stitch around the side and top edges with red embroidery floss (thread). Place the stockings and mittens in the gap between the two layers to make sure they fit.

4 Cut six 20-in. (50-cm) lengths of red-
and-white baker's twine. Fold each
one in half and tie the loose ends in a
knot. Thread the twine onto the plastic
tapestry needle. Gently push the needle
up through the cuff between two blanket
stitches in the top right-hand corner.

5 Place the mittens and stockings in
their respective cuffs. Using white
thread, machine stitch across the bottom
of each cuff.

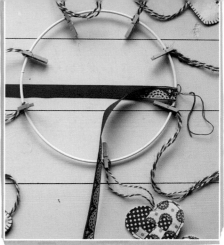

6 To attach the hearts, cut a 28-in. (70-cm) length of twine. Fold it in half and tie the ends together, as before. Using the tapestry needle, attach a clear bead to the end. Space the hearts evenly on the twine (mark their positions with a pencil if necessary). Using white thread, work a few machine stitches across the top and bottom of each heart to attach it to the twine.

7 Assemble your mobile by looping the twine hanging strings around the metal hoop, as shown in the photo. To keep them in place, add a small wooden clothespin on top of each loop. It's not just helpful—they're really pretty, too!

8 To make the "holder" for the mobile, cut 48-in. (120-cm) lengths of red-and-white ribbon. Place one length horizontally under the metal hoop and pull it so that the two ends meet when you hold them up in front of you, making sure each side has equal length of ribbon. Secure each side with a few stitches, using red thread.

9 Remove the length of twine holding the three hearts. Attach the second ribbon vertically in the same way as the first, then hand stitch a small "X" over the point where the two ribbons overlap in the center of the hoop to fix them in place.

10 Gather the four ribbon ends together in your hand and hold them in the air above the metal hoop. Tie them in a knot, making sure all four strips are pulled tight. Take two ribbon ends in each hand and make a large bow. Snip the ribbon ends diagonally to give the bow a pretty finish.

11 Attach the twine holding the three hearts to the front ribbon with a small wooden clothespin. To add a little more Christmas magic, sew one shape of wooden button to each type of motif, using red sewing thread.

Forest friends
CHRISTMAS STOCKING

In preparation for Christmas there are plenty of beautiful things you can make by hand to add a true homemade feel to your home. Here's a sweet Christmas stocking to hang on the mantelpiece, inspired by my own childhood in the midst of a deep Scandinavian forest. Even though I love every season in its own way, seeing the animals in winter when out playing with my sisters was so very special and it gave me lifelong memories to treasure.

YOU WILL NEED

- Templates on page 125
- ¾ yd (70 cm) thick natural or light beige cotton canvas, 44 in. (112 cm) wide
- Scraps of yellow, green, white, black, red and orange felt
- Natural ric-rac braid 5½ in. (14 cm) long
- 5 in. (12 cm) ribbon to match the cotton canvas, ⅜ in. (1 cm) wide
- 4 dark brown and 2 black seed beads
- Sewing threads to match the cotton canvas and felt colors
- Basic kit (see page 120)

TOP TIP

If your fabric has patterns or lines, make sure they align front and back!

1 Copy the stocking template on page 125 and cut it out. Fold the cotton canvas in half, pin the template to it, and cut out two stocking shapes. Fold over ⅜ in. (1 cm) along the top of each stocking piece, press, and machine stitch.

2 Like many of my fellow Scandinavians, I suffer from the so-called "Compulsive Cookie Cutter Collector Syndrome"! I have eight boxes full of them, and am constantly looking out for new ones. You can either use the templates on page 125 or use your own cookie cutters to cut out three green Christmas trees in different shapes and sizes from green felt and a golden sun (using a star or snowflake cutter) to shine over the wintery landscape.

3 Place the trees near the bottom of one stocking piece and sew in place with green sewing thread, making sure you leave enough room on the sides for the seam allowance (at least ⅝ in./1.5 cm). Sew the yellow sun to the top of the stocking, using matching thread.

4 Now we need to add a few little forest friends to the design. Using the templates, cut out a fox's head from orange felt and a badger's face from white felt. Sew them just above the trees, using matching thread as before.

5 Give the animals their defining features—the fox his white cheeks and red eyebrows, and the badger his beautiful black face stripes. The forest friends will also need eyes and noses, so add two brown seed beads for eyes and a black one for a nose, using black sewing thread.

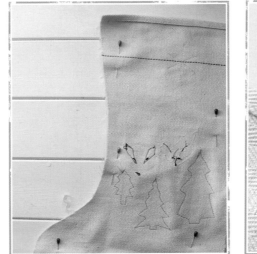

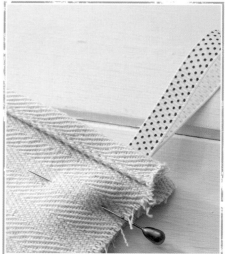

6 Draw a pencil line across the middle of the toe and cut a length of ric-rac braid a little longer than the sock toe is wide. Stitch the ric-rac in place using neutral sewing thread. Trim all loose threads on all the appliquéd decorations.

7 Pin the two stocking pieces right sides together. Cut a 4-in. (10-cm) length of ribbon, fold it in half to make a loop, and pin it in the top right-hand corner, just in from the edge. Sew around the stocking, taking a ⅜-in. (1-cm) seam allowance and leaving the top edge open but sewing the ribbon loop. Remove all the pins.

8 Trim all loose thread ends and turn the stocking right side out, gently pushing out the seams of the stocking to make sure you haven't missed stitching anywhere. Press the stocking and hang it up for everyone to see!

TOOLS AND TECHNIQUES

BASIC KIT

The projects in this book can all be made with very little equipment. A basic kit is listed below; any other tools and equipment are mentioned in the "You will need" list at the start of each project.

• Tracing, copy, or parchment paper for tracing the templates on pages 122–125.

• A long ruler, a flexible measuring tape, and a pencil or tailor's chalk for measuring and marking fabric and drawing around templates.

• Scissors reserved especially for cutting out paper templates.

• Dressmaker's shears for cutting fabric. Never, ever use your dressmaking shears for cutting paper, as this will quickly blunt them.

• Small, sharp-pointed scissors for cutting threads, clipping seam allowances, and trimming.

• Pinking shears for cutting around the edges of appliqué shapes to prevent them from fraying.

• Dressmaker's pins for pinning paper templates in place and pinning pieces together while you sew them. It's also worth having some long pins for when you need to pin several thicker layers of fabric together—for example, the Child's Sami-Inspired Slippers on page 72, where you have to pin two sole pieces together with a layer of batting (wadding) sandwiched in between.

• Hand-sewing needles and embroidery needles; the type of embroidery needle depends on the fabric and thread you are using. Sharp-pointed needles called crewels are thin, but are designed to take thicker-than-normal thread and are ideal

for most decorative embroidery on plain-weave fabrics. Chenilles are sharp-pointed and heavier, and take thicker threads for work on heavyweight fabrics.

• A sewing machine is essential, but it can be a very simple model. Even the most basic of modern sewing machines offers a variety of stitches. For this book, you will only need straight stitch and, perhaps, zigzag stitch.

• A steam iron and ironing board are essential for pressing seams, and also for applying iron-on interfacing to fabrics to stiffen them and fusible bonding web to fuse two layers of fabric together.

FABRICS AND THREADS

I have used natural fabrics in all the projects, especially linen and cotton, many of which I have found during my highly enjoyable searches through various Scandinavian flea markets, but you can find wonderfully Nordic material in the suppliers list on page 126. I also used wool felt for many projects. This can be difficult to source, but you can easily replace it with acrylic felt. Panduro Hobby has a large and colorful selection.

The other essential is sewing thread. Ideally, try to match the thread type to the fabric (synthetic thread for synthetic fabric, cotton thread for cotton fabric) and match the thread color as closely as possible to the fabric color.

For most of the embroidery in this book, I have used stranded embroidery floss (thread). I usually use two strands only.

CHANGING THE SIZE OF MOTIFS

The project instructions and the templates on pages 122–125 specify how much you need to enlarge motifs in order for your project to be the same size as the ones I made, but you may well wish to adapt a design to make something completely different—so it's worth knowing how to enlarge or reduce motifs to the size you want.

Enlarging motifs

• First, decide how big you want the pattern or motif to be. Let's say that you want a particular shape to be 10 in. (25 cm) tall.

• Then measure the template that you are working from—5 in. (12.5 cm) tall, for example.

• Take the size that you want the pattern or motif to be (10 in./25 cm) and divide it by the actual size of the template (5 in./12.5 cm). Multiply that figure by 100 and you get 200—so you need to enlarge the motif on a photocopier to 200 percent.

Reducing motifs

If you want a motif on the finished piece to be smaller than the template in this book, the process is exactly the same. For example, if the pattern is 5 in. (12.5 cm) tall and you want the motif to be 3 in. (7.5 cm) tall, divide 3 in./7.5 cm by the actual size of the template (5 in./12.5 cm) and multiply by 100, which gives you a figure of 60. So the figure that you need to key in on the photocopier is 60 percent.

HAND STITCHES

There are many hand stitches; this section shows the ones I used in the projects, but you can, of course, substitute stitches of your own choice.

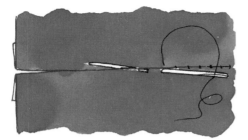

Slipstitch

Slipstitch is used to close openings—for example, when you've left a gap in a seam in order to turn a piece right side out—and to appliqué one piece of fabric to another. Work from right to left. Slide the needle between the two pieces of fabric, bringing it out on the edge of the top fabric so that the knot in the thread is hidden between the two layers. Pick up one or two threads from the base fabric, then bring the needle up a short distance along, on the edge of the top fabric, and pull through. Repeat to the end.

Backstitch

Work from right to left. Bring the needle up from the back of the fabric, one stitch length to the left of the end of the stitching line. Insert it one stitch length to the right, at the very end of the stitching line, and bring it up again one stitch length in front of the point from which it first emerged. Pull the thread through. To begin the next stitch, insert the needle at the left-hand end of the previous stitch. Continue to the end.

Fern stitch

Bring the needle to the front of the fabric at A and put it in at B. Bring the needle out at C and put it in at B. Then bring it out again at D and again put it in at B to complete the stitch. Bring the needle out just below B to continue.

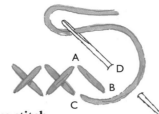

Cross stitch

To work a single cross stitch, bring the needle up at A and down at B, then up at C and down at D.

To work a row of cross stitches, work the diagonal stitches in one direction only, from right to left, then reverse the direction and work the second half of the stitch across each stitch made on the first journey.

French knot

Bring the needle up from the back of the fabric to the front. Wrap the thread two or three times around the tip of the needle, then reinsert the needle at the point where it first emerged, holding the wrapped threads with the thumbnail of your non-stitching hand, and pull the needle all the way through. The wraps will form a knot on the surface of the fabric.

Satin stitch

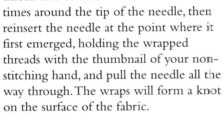

This is a "filling" stitch that is useful for motifs such as flower petals and leaves. Work from left to right. Draw the shape on the fabric, then work straight stitches across it, coming up at A and down at B, then up at C, and so on. Place the stitches next to each other, so that no fabric can be seen between them. You can also work a row of backstitch around the edge to define the outline more clearly.

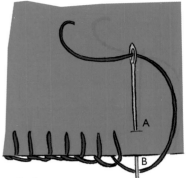

Blanket stitch

Bring the needle out at the edge of the fabric. Insert the needle at A, to the right and above the edge, then bring it down to the edge of the fabric at B, keeping the thread under the needle tip. Draw the needle through to form a looped stitch.

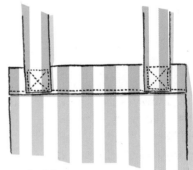

Box stitching

There's one bit of machine stitching that's really useful for strengthening the ends of straps or when you're joining two ends of elastic together in a casing. As the name suggests, box stitching simply means stitching in a box shape with a cross in the center. It is used wherever a strong, reinforced join is needed—for example, when attaching straps to bags.

Starting at one edge, machine stitch across the strap in a square, finishing with the needle down in the fabric. Pivot the work around the needle and stitch diagonally across the square to the opposite corner, then along the side of the square over the first line of stitching, and finally diagonally across the square to the opposite corner.

TEMPLATES

All the templates will need to be enlarged and the easiest way is on a photocopier—the percentage enlargement is 200%. See page 120 for instructions on changing the size of motifs.

Nordic mugwarmers
page 12

Nordic coasters
page 12

Striped cotton bread basket
page 20

Kurbits-style doorstop
page 35

Folklore flower pillow
page 17

Nordic folklore bunting
page 38

Tasseled heart trio
page 28

Braided half apron page 42
Scandi laptop cover page 52

Dala horse diary
page 46

Cool-blue iPad cover
page 63

Strap end curve

Large leaf

Small leaf

Heart

Over-the-shoulder bag
page 66

Lingonberry bag
page 56

Side

Sole

Dala horse earphone tidy
page 60

Child's Sami-inspired slippers
page 72

Love birds mobile
page 96

Norwegian forest kittens
page 82

Lynx

Wild boar

Child's felt bag
page 78

Squirrel

Toadstool

Tree

Matchbox pets
page 92

Child's vintage apron
page 85

Badger

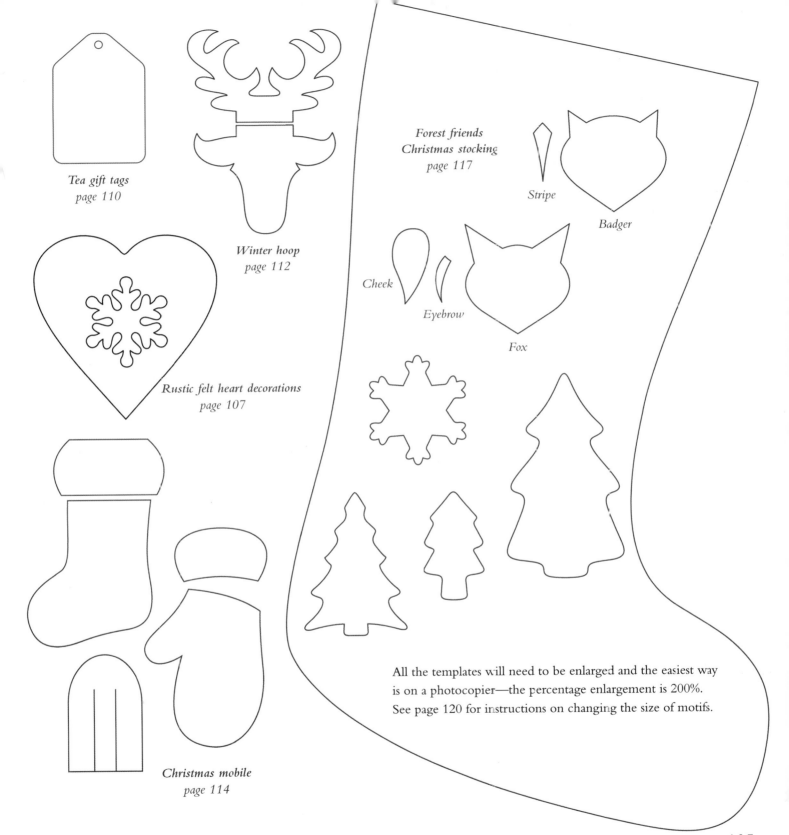

Tea gift tags
page 110

Winter hoop
page 112

Rustic felt heart decorations
page 107

Christmas mobile
page 114

Forest friends
Christmas stocking
page 117

Stripe

Badger

Cheek

Eyebrow

Fox

All the templates will need to be enlarged and the easiest way
is on a photocopier—the percentage enlargement is 200%.
See page 120 for instructions on changing the size of motifs.

SUPPLIERS

UK SUPPLIERS

Blooming Felt
www.bloomingfelt.co.uk

The Cloth House
47 Berwick Street
London W1F 8SL
020 7437 5155
www.clothhouse.com

Dots n Stripes
www.dotsnstripes.co.uk

Duttons for Buttons
www.duttonsforbuttons.co.uk

Hus & Hem
The Design Quarter
12 High Street
Ledbury
Herefordshire HR8 1DS
01531 631044
www.husandhem.co.uk

John Lewis
Stores nationwide
03456 049 049
www.johnlewis.com

LinenMe
www.linenme.com

MacCulloch and Wallis
25–26 Poland Street
London WIF 8QN
020 7629 0311
www.macculloch-wallis.co.uk

Ian Mankin
269/273 Wandsworth Bridge Road
London SW6 2TX
020 7722 0997
www.ianmankin.co.uk

Panduro Hobby
www.pandurohobby.co.uk

V V Rouleaux
102 Marylebone Lane
London W1U 2QD
020 7224 5179
www.vvrouleaux.com

The Swedish Fabric Company
www.theswedishfabriccompany.com

Tinsmiths
Tinsmiths Alley
8A High Street
Ledbury
Herefordshire HR8 1DS
01531 632083
www.tinsmiths.co.uk

US SUPPLIERS

Amy Butler
www.amybutlerdesign.com

Britex Fabrics
146 Geary Street
San Francisco, CA 94108
415-392-2910
www.britexfabrics.com

Buy Fabrics
8967 Rand Avenue
Daphne, Al 36526
877-625-2889
www.buyfabrics.com

Cia's Palette
4155 Grand Avenue S
Minneapolis, MN 55409
612-229-5228
www.ciaspalette.com

Discount Fabrics USA
108 N. Carroll Street.
Thurmont, MD 21788
301-271-2266
discountfabricsusacorp.com

DoxieShop.com
www.doxieshop.com

FabDir.com
The Internet's largest fabric store
directory
www.fabdir.com

Fabricland/Fabricville
Over 170 stores in Canada and the U.S.
www.fabricland.com
www.fabricville.com

Hobby Lobby
Stores nationwide
www.hobbylobby.com

Ikea
www.ikea.com/us

J & O Fabrics
9401 South Crescent Blvd.
Pennsauken, NJ 08110
856-663-2121
www.jandofabrics.com

Jo-Ann Fabric and Craft Store
Stores nationwide
1-888-739-4120
www.joann.com

Lucy's Fabrics
103 S. College Street
Anna, TX 75409
972-924-8080
www.lucysfabrics.com

**Marimekko Upper East Side
NY/Kiitos Marimekko**
1262 Third Avenue (Between 72nd and
73rd Streets)
New York, NY 10021
800 527-0624
www.kiitosmarimekko.com

Michaels
Stores nationwide
1-800-642-4235
www.michaels.com

Purl Soho
459 Broome Street
New York, NY 10013
212-420-8796
www.purlsoho.com

Vogue Fabrics
718-732 Main Street
Evanston, IL 60202
847-864-9600

INDEX

ACKNOWLEDGMENTS

First, I would like to extend a huge and heartfelt thank you to CICO Books for having faith in me and for giving me this wonderful opportunity to put my creations into print and bring them to life. My gratitude goes especially to Cindy Richards, Penny Craig, Miriam Catley, Sarah Hoggett, Geoff Borin, Penny Wincer, and Nel Haynes, for their guidance and expertise in creating such a beautiful book!

A very, very special thank you and I love you to my wonderful family—my husband Patrick and children Tom, Finn, and Lily. I thank you for your never-ending support, patience, and encouragement. You are my love, my life, and my fire!

To my three dearest sisters, Lina, Hanna, and Maja; I wouldn't want to go a single day of this life without you three by my side. All for one and one for all!

Thank you to my father for letting me loose in his workshop as a child.

To my mother, Irene—she went away far too soon. I would have loved for her to see this book—she would have been so thrilled.

And to Lotta, my fourth and unofficial sister—you're my rock.

My range of Scandinavian handmade interior decorations is now available on www.thenorthernshores.com